SECOND FIDDLES

Prime Examples of Strength in the Shadows

By Paul C. Cline, PhD

Print: 979-8-218-15956-6
EPUB: 979-8-218-15957-3

Published by The Literary Spa

To Diane and our growing family

Contents

The Second Fiddle

It's all about the leader. They are the ones who are seen, followed, sought after, worshipped, and adored. They make the history books. They are studied in academies, training programs, and classes. They head up the nations, corporations, universities, departments, and offices. Their names are in the titles of books, plays, television programs. They are it.

And they deserve the attention they get. After all, the leaders are turned to for vision, creativity, and...leadership. The buck stops with them. They are responsible for whatever they are connected with, and subject to, and even sometimes blindsided by, criticism for mistakes they make or are made by those responsible to them. They get the sleepless nights and the ulcers.

But maybe, from a certain point of view, it's not *all* about them. Seldom does a leader run the program, lead the enterprise, or carry the whole play all by themselves. There are almost always the others. The lesser lights. The little people.

And usually there is one who also carries a big part of the load, maybe even more of the load than the leader. Any load of any size requires sharing. It is important to have someone to share the task with someone who is capable, loyal, and energetic, and who is satisfied to take on perhaps a big part of the task—and who is willing not to be the leader.

Why would anyone agree to do this—do the work in the shadow of another? This is a basic question to be answered in this book. At first blush it seems strange and even wrong that someone would have their shoulder to the wheel and not be the focus of attention, admiration, and remuneration.

Another question. What are these aides like? How capable are they? They must have some strengths, or they would not be very useful. Are their strengths similar to, distinguishable from, or complementary to those of the leader?

Are there ever occasions when the assistant in some way leads the leader? Hardly anyone can be so vital in all areas as never to benefit from some guidance, admonishment, or prodding. Does it depend upon the nature of the leader as to whether the aide gets away with or is appreciated for taking at least a tentative hold of the reins?

What effect do outside forces, such as circumstances, funding, or other strong individuals have upon the relationship of the leader and the associate? Enterprises do not exist in a vacuum. What is their top dogs' connection with forces they cannot control?

As we consider the main characters in the various fictional and non-fictional endeavors that we encounter, we might call the leader the Principal. What of the primary assistant? Aide, associate, second banana? Or maybe—Second Fiddle.

What might cause a person to be a Second Fiddle?
Since "it's all about the leader," what would motivate an individual to take on a position of responsibility that would be subservient to another? Further, why would that individual remain subservient to another over an extend-

ed period of time, perhaps never seeking or accepting the position of Principal?

Loyalty may not be as far-fetched as our cynical society would proclaim today.

But would loyalty be enough to cause a person to work beneath another? Perhaps, if that loyalty were of the type that would motivate that individual. And there are probably numerous forms of allegiance.

This allegiance might stem from an affection, or a high respect for the leader or some other person who is influential upon the Second Fiddle. For example, Bobby Kennedy helped his brother Jack as campaign manager and member of his cabinet at least to some extent at the bidding of Joseph Kennedy, their father.

The tradition of a family in politics also played a part in Bobby's setting aside his own plans to accommodate the family's goals. Tradition could likewise be a factor in business or education or other family field of endeavor. Both of Bobby's grandfathers had been Massachusetts pols.

Love could explain a spouse's long-term support during a career that causes bumps in the marriage and aggravation if not hardship for both. In politics, the husband or wife might be held up to criticism by opponents or the public. In business, it might be the need to entertain or associate with those one can barely tolerate. In volunteerism, it might be going without some of the "good things in life," and depriving children of the best that one desires for them.

Of course, the limelight might be a sufficient prod for the Second Fiddle to sign on for duty. The honor, activities, and fun surrounding the leader would likely extend to the top associate. The Second Fiddle might not get the award, but would be there when it was received. They might not get the spotlight, but would be there when the lights were turned up. This could be enough to satisfy many Second Fiddles.

Money is a powerful draw, even if one has to work for another, even perform the work of the Principal. The Principal is well taken care of and, as they advance in salary and perquisites, so does the Second Fiddle. That might cause the aide to continue on those particularly difficult days. Finances have been the cause of the inception of the Principal and Second Fiddle's initial contact. This was the case when Sherlock Holmes and Dr. Watson were introduced by a mutual acquaintance so that they might share lodging at 221B Baker Street, London.

Money also may provide security where it is a good bet that the Principal is firmly established and will be on the job or a higher position for a good long time. The Second Fiddle will not have to move, or find another position, which is a lot of trouble and can cause anxiety about the future.

Anxiety might be a symptom of a personality that motivates the Second Fiddle. Not just the trouble of finding another position, the fear of what that move might result in—possibly a less secure, less desirable, less satisfying situation. Certainty here, even in the face of admitted drawbacks and problems, may be better than tackling the unknown.

The psychological make-up of the Principal has been studied extensively over the years. Head-hunters evidently have a handle on the characteristics of an individual that would fit them for a position of responsibility. Why wouldn't there be identifiable attributes in the personality of the Second Fiddle? Consideration will be given to these attributes while exploring the relationship of the Second

Fiddle to the Principal. For instance, what place does shyness have in the perennial service by an associate? Do some individuals just not like to have ultimate responsibility—having the buck stop with them? Do some persons like the feeling of power when representing the Principal and issuing orders on their behalf?

Possibly the Second Fiddle would wish to use their closeness to the Principal to further their own agenda, as in the case of Eleanor Roosevelt in pursuing, while Franklin was President, the policies in which she was interested. Their marriage reputedly had become less based upon affection than upon mutual performance of tasks important to the other.

Apparently the motivations supporting the Second Fiddle's assumption of the job and the continuance to serve are many. Perhaps it will be discovered that these purposes vary at least slightly for one Principal and Second Fiddle relationship to the next. It may be concluded, however, that certain needs are met and desires satisfied throughout most of these associations.

What are Second Fiddles like?

They presumably are loyal, and have a personality that permits or thrives upon subservience. They are capable of performing their duties, maintain confidences well, and are honest and stable.

Even a preliminary look at Second Fiddles that come immediately to mind indicates that it is difficult to make general rules for this class of individuals. Just a look at the above characteristics will reveal that it's not as simple as all that.

For instance, to take the first point, often the Second Fiddle did not seek their present position. Possibly they were looking for something more, maybe even the typical dream job of being in charge, responsible to no one. The relationship may, rather than planned, be a result of happenstance, as Tonto's saving the life of the young man who was to become the Lone Ranger. They are probably loyal, but it is not unknown for the assistant to be plotting to take the Principal's position. The Second Fiddle may find that they do not have the temperament to have a position lower than being completely in charge. They may find that the Principal is not as competent or, because of some unpleasant trait, not worthy of devotion.

Presumably they are at least reasonably capable in serving the Principal, but things can happen. They may be assigned additional duties for which they are not suited, or for which they have a distaste. They may not keep up with the advances in their field, perhaps because information comes to the Principal but not to them.

The traits of keeping secrets, honesty, and stability, while attributable to the best of the Second Fiddles, are subject to varying conditions on the job. The person in the shadows may tire of being taken for granted. The secrets may be of a nature as to test one's ethical principles. Sometimes one may be called upon to lie "for the good of the team." These and other conditions can adversely affect the stability of the Second Fiddle in the relationship with the Principal.

The look into a variety of Second Fiddle-Principal relationships will reveal other characteristics and the situations where the apparent rules will be called into question. One of these may be where the Second Fiddle has responsibility for administering a large number of people on behalf of the Principal. What is their role then? They may be more leader in some ways than second in command.

Who are the Second Fiddles?

If one but thinks for a moment, they will recall several combinations of leaders and prime supporters whom we are calling Principals and Second Fiddles. These entities are found in fiction as well as real life. The advantage of the fictional creation is that the product may be more dramatic than one might find in reality. The fictional track also permits the inclusion of the mystery, often with the combination of the detective and sidekick.

In the real world the realm of politics furnishes a host of associations. Some arise in family situations, such as between brothers Robert and John Kennedy, and between married individuals, such as Eleanor and Franklin Roosevelt.

Where there are leaders with staff positions beneath them one finds a fertile field for Second Fiddles. This applies not only to the executive and legislative branches of government, but also to corporations, nonprofit organizations, and other business structures.

Various strains of religious heritage offer individuals who serve others. Old Testament figures include Ruth and Naomi, and brothers Aaron and Moses. The New Testament yields Timothy and Paul, among others.

Sports teams bear consideration from the standpoint of assistants and the coach, pitching coaches and managers, and associates of such officers as athletic directors and general managers. Certain positions in sports, such as the football quarterback, may give rise to a leadership position that would on occasion attract a second fiddle.

A couple of caveats are worth noting. That is the temptation to categorize as a Second Fiddle, someone who is merely an associate of another. For instance, Lou Gehrig performed partially under the shadow of the great Babe Ruth, but Gehrig did not serve Ruth. Some would even argue that there was not a wide divide in the abilities of the two baseball greats.

One could also easily fall into stereotypical traps in the analysis of relationships. Differences in gender, race, ethnicity, and the like does not lead necessarily to the placement of an individual into the category of Second Fiddle. In fact, in the example of the Roosevelts, the level of the contributions of Eleanor during and after the marriage was possibly sufficient to belie the position of secondary status.

The selection of Principals and Second Fiddles to highlight is challenging. Each reader would likely come up with a different list, based upon likes and dislikes, politics, favorite characters in literature, and a variety of other subjective criteria. Included in the following pages are descriptions of characters, real and fictional, from one such list. It would be difficult to fully justify each selection, particularly in light of other Second Fiddles eminently worthy of being chosen.

Luckily, the goal here is to look at the relationship of the leader and their significant supporter, and not to include an exhaustive parade of examples of these combinations. An attempt is made to include sufficient variety to spotlight the interactions. At the same time almost any list of Principals and Second Fiddles yields fascinating characters in dramatic situations, as the next several chapters will show.

1

Eleanor Roosevelt and FDR

She was often mistaken, not often blind,
And she knew the whole duty of womankind,
To take the burden and have the power,
And seem like the well-protected flower...

From "John Brown's Body," by Stephen Vincent Benet

It would be too much to expect that all the elements in Benet's description would fit perfectly such a unique individual as Eleanor, a Roosevelt, and the wife of America's President. But we may initially suggest that the terms of the rhyme apply rather well, with the exception of the first and the last, the matter of being often mistaken and a well-protected flower. We shall see how the evidence bears out the accuracy of each of these attributes.

And we shall consider the evidence to determine the accuracy of suggesting that Eleanor is the Second Fiddle to Franklin's Principal. Their relationship of husband and wife was complex enough; added to that was the Depression and war-time tribulations that affected each of them in many ways.

Both public and personal considerations gave rise to the uniqueness of this combination of President and First Lady. Of all the anomalies in the lives of Eleanor Roosevelt and Franklin Delano Roosevelt the most graphic example was Franklin's walking in spite of the well-known fact that he could not walk. He performed this very arduous feat, of course, by locking the braces on his polio-immobilized legs, standing, and, leaning on the arm of a strong son, moved his lower limbs in a semi-circular motion to approximate walking.

Other paradoxes were less visible but equally as important in the Roosevelts' relationship with each other. He was the most-often-elected and powerful crises president. Even though she held no office and played down any significant public stature, she was often selected as one of the most influential Americans. Even though she worked largely to further Franklin's career, she was mentioned at various times as an appropriate candidate for either vice president or president.

Another oddity: They were each born to different strands of the same wealthy and prominent New York State family. Their forebears had played leading social and economic roles in both Manhattan and the Hudson Valley. While the family frowned upon engaging in political activity, one of their own, Theodore had been President of the United States. In the light of this heritage it was not strange that the young couple had three servants when they embarked upon married life in their New York City apartment. In spite of this background of prestige and elite status both influenced the other to assume the task of helping the less fortunate of their day. Even during World War II Eleanor fretted that the social agenda of the government was falling behind and continued to push for help for returning service personnel as well as those who could not meet their basic needs.

And also for Eleanor, since she held no office, there was the problem of attempting to secure an ambitious agenda for the country without seeming to "not know her place," and without upsetting the president while at the same time going through him for support for her proposals.

Hopefully, these and other strange features of their complex personalities and relationship will become clearer by a look at how they began and how their marriage and careers developed.

Cousins

They met for the first time as small children and thereafter at family gatherings. Her mother was a Hall and their bent was upon duty and propriety. She was a rather unapproachable person for Eleanor and was often uncharitable in her approach to her daughter, calling her "Granny" on one occasion. Perhaps Eleanor at least partially earned the name because of her choice of duty over enjoyment. Anna Hall died when Eleanor was ten and she went to live with her grandmother Hall.

Eleanor's father, Elliott, was a brother of the president, Theodore. Elliott and Anna Hall were leading lights in New York City society. Unfortunately, Elliott died when Eleanor was eight, but was a very dear, warm father. He represented his branch of the Roosevelts in his joyousness; however, his mental condition deteriorated to depression and the severe abuse of alcohol, to the extent that he was for a time institutionalized and left for a time to work in Virginia. His wish for Eleanor was, among other things, that she be brave, studious, and good.

Grandmother Hall sent Eleanor to the Allenwood School near London. This school stressed openness to new ideas and working for the good of society. As a result of this schooling and her upbringing she incorporated consideration of others and a will to succeed.

Franklin was a highly ambitious young man, charming, and popular with the girls. He tended to have a positive outlook on life, based upon the security that both family wealth and a prestigious name had granted him. His mother Sara was a decided influence upon him throughout much of his life. Sara was a Delano, also one of the first families of New York State. She had an adventurous youth, even going with her father to China for his business interests there. Franklin's father, James, was fifty-two when he married Sara, twice her age. Franklin indicated some early maturity when he tended to James when he became ill.

Sara's life as a widow revolved around Franklin. She was ever present in her son and daughter-in-law's life, to the extent of buying them homes near hers and attempting to influence their children. She resented the marriage to Eleanor but went along in an effort to remain close to Franklin. Franklin and Eleanor both felt put upon by the hovering Sara, but it was not until later in their marriage that they rebelled to claim their privacy and independence. A major hold that Sara had over the couple was her generosity in providing them with the money to have a life in society and raise their children in a manner that would not be possible if they relied upon their individual wealth.

Drawn to the plain, shy Eleanor who wanted someone to care for and find security with, Franklin was happy to have found a strong woman to help him in attaining his ambitions. They were married March 17, 1900. Their honeymoon was a week at Hyde Park on the Hudson, as Franklin was in Harvard Law School. Later, they took a three month European tour.

The couple moved with their three servants into a New York City apartment rented by Sara that was near her own. With the help of Sara's money they were part of the lively City social scene. They were also interested in public affairs, Franklin through ambition and Eleanor, at least publicly, because of a wife's supposed duty to support her husband's endeavors.

When Franklin sought the office of state senator and won, Eleanor found that she liked being a public figure's wife, although she was hesitant to admit it. She had previously worked in the New York City settlement houses as a member of the Junior League and had been interested in the issues of the day, perhaps following the admonition of Uncle Theodore that young people give of themselves for the public good.

Franklin was long on action but short on a philosophy on which to base his political career. Eleanor fulfilled the role of sharpening his outlook on the issues coming before him for decision. It was a two-way street, however, since he was the one who persuaded her to support women's suffrage.

Washington life

In the election of 1912 they split their support for president. He chose to help Woodrow Wilson, mirroring his branch of the family's Democratic leanings, while she supported her Uncle Theodore. When Wilson won, Franklin was offered the position of Assistant Secretary of the Navy.

He settled into his new job in Washington and she worked hard to do the things expected of the wife of a national official, in addition to giving birth to five sons and a daughter. Five of the children lived to reach maturity. She enthusiastically engaged in the ritual of calling on the wives of other high government officers and being "at home" certain times of the day for their visits. During the

First World War she headed a Navy Department's knitting project and gave leadership to a canteen for service personnel. The War provided her with an opportunity to have independent roles in the public arena which she enjoyed and at which she was competent. The War increased her confidence to accept challenges outside of the home just as the conflict changed the outlook of the women who had contributed so much to the war effort.

To assist Eleanor in the position of social secretary, a young woman, Lucy Mercer, came to the Roosevelt home. In 1918 while unpacking Franklin's bags after a trip, Eleanor found love letters to her husband from Lucy. This revelation caused a major change in Eleanor and her relationship with her husband. The incident caused her to experience severe depression and self-doubt.

The trauma of the incident made Eleanor consider her future role. She remained with Franklin, and she supported him as the good, dutiful wife, but they were no longer intimate during their married life. She became more independent, focusing more on her individual interests and goals. For instance, she gave time to organized efforts to improve the lot of women workers, especially African-Americans and immigrants. Her independence extended to her relationship with Franklin's mother, Sara, who had until then been an ever-present part of their lives.

A major adviser to Franklin was Louis Howe, a former newspaperman. Howe convinced her that her warm personality and other attributes could be important in Franklin's unsuccessful campaign for vice-president in 1920. He coached her in her public speaking, toning down her high-pitched voice and giving her confidence in her abilities in politics.

Howe was the first of the many key advisers to whom Franklin turned during his long career in government. His relationship with Eleanor remained good until the end of his life through Franklin's various campaigns and offices. In spite of the fact that they were both Second Fiddles to Franklin's Principal, or leadership, they seemed to mesh in their support rather than be in conflict.

This natural cooperation with another Second Fiddle was not the norm for Eleanor through the ensuing years. Rather, she typically became a self-advocate with the individuals upon whom Franklin closely relied, in order to pursue her own goals and the interests which others wanted furthered. She would accomplish this advocacy by various means. Sometimes she would indicate that Franklin wished something to be done. Sometimes she would suggest that a position be taken, with the implication the idea was her husband's. She used her direct contact with Franklin to persuade him to move in a certain direction. Sometimes she used indirection by asking him how she should respond to a letter or a request by a constituent.

More and more the couple went their separate ways. Eleanor, having changed from Republican to Democrat, took on roles in political campaigns and worked for women and children's rights with organizations such as the League of Women Voters. She was a teetotaler and supported Prohibition, while Franklin was not nearly so much a "dry." She was an advocate for peace and the betterment of mankind.

Polio

In 1921 Franklin was changed by polio from a vital, healthy person to a life-long cripple. He could no longer use his legs, and was required to utilize heavy braces in order to stand. Eleanor was his dedicated nurse, as well as secretary.

She believed that he should continue an active life and refused to permit him to give in to his handicap. She invited political associates to the home, helped him continue his correspondence, and paved the way for his eventual return to public life. She made appearances on his behalf and continued to accept responsibilities in the Democratic Party, particularly in organizing women to participate and vote.

The "Flapper Age" advanced further the independence of women, and Eleanor grew in confidence as she stood in for Franklin until he could stand for office on his own. Franklin made plans and she carried them out. They supported Al Smith for New York Governor.

In seeking greater comfort and at least some relief from the effects of polio, Franklin spent time away from Eleanor, first in the warm waters of Florida, then in Warm Springs, Georgia, which he eventually purchased and dedicated to helping other polio victims. He was accompanied on his trips to Florida by "Missy" LeGrande, an assistant with whom it has been suggested he was romantically attached. At Warm Springs and later at the White House he continued seeing Lucy Mercer, who had become Mrs. Rutherford, even to the time of his death. Eleanor at first, at least, trusted Missy in her assisting Franklin, but the fact that the relationship with Lucy continued was kept from her by staff, friends, and family.

Eleanor stepped up her independent interests, partnering and teaching in a New York City private school, Todhunter, off Park Avenue, and building, with friends, Val-Kill Cottage on Franklin's land near the Hyde Park home, possibly to get away from Franklin's mother. With the same friends she established Val-Kill industries for the promotion and sale of local Duchess County, New York, products. She was active in radio and in lecturing.

Governor

Contrary to the opinion of Louis Howe, she believed Franklin to be sufficiently strong to run for governor of New York in 1928. He won the election, while she, as usual, did not campaign, but worked behind the scenes. This refraining from public view was perhaps her natural inclination, but it also reflected the various "binds" that Second Fiddles similar to her, as the non-elected spouse of an officeholder, find themselves. Even though she had become a significant figure in the state, politics was still thought to be a man's activity, and no place for a woman. As a result she had to appear that she was uninterested in the political wars.

Further, as Franklin's wife, her position had typically been one of anonymity so as not to be looked at as interfering with his work, or worse, directing him in various political decisions. She had to be careful not to impinge on the realm of Franklin's various advisers, often Second Fiddles in their own right.

In spite of her care in remaining anonymous and in deferring to her husband publicly, as a bright individual with experience and positions on various public issues, she did exert influence over Franklin by raising such matters as wages for minorities and assistance for families. She urged the appointment of women to posts in state government and in general supported women's issues.

This acting as a "spur," as she called it, was not always welcomed by Franklin. He would sometimes, especially in later years, rebel against her suggestions and seek to get away from her, while at the same time relying on her judgment, especially in matters relating to the well-being of the people.

The political union may not have been the only force that held them together. When she died, among her papers was found with the notation "1918" the following lines from the poem "Psyche," by Virginia Moore: "The soul that has believed/and was deceived/ends by believing more/than ever before."

Among Eleanor's independent actions was an intimate affair with Lorena Hickok, known as "Hick." She was a reporter who became Eleanor's closest friend.

In spite of this and possibly other relationships with women, Eleanor still considered herself as a "man's woman," devoted to Franklin until the end of his days.

In the governorship and in other office-holding Franklin leaned more to career goals, doing what was necessary, sometimes avoiding difficult decisions. From his experiences with polio and with the less-well-off around Warm Springs, he did develop a compassion for the plight of others. He often kept his thoughts to himself, leaving Eleanor out of the picture. Eleanor favored activity and working for others even when it was sometimes necessary to break some rules.

While Franklin was governor, Eleanor added another dimension to her role as helpmeet. She traveled the state of New York and inspected the various public facilities. She then reported back to Franklin. She performed a similar role as her husband's "legs" while he was president, not only in peacetime but also in visiting the troops in various theaters of action throughout the world.

The Presidency

Franklin became president in 1933 with the help of Eleanor. She helped in securing the nomination and her involvement in the women's division of the party. Perhaps no longer truly in love with him, she worked strenuously for the things that he sought. This was in spite of the fact that she did not wish to give up her rather independent life in New York for what she believed would be stifling life in the White House. As a result, she fell into a sort of depression.

She soon found that she could be helpful to Franklin in Washington, however, and, at the urging of Hick, she began holding news conferences for women of the press as well as the traditional entertaining and other activities of first ladies.

But, in the mode of a true Second Fiddle, she was more. Concerned that advisers would not give Franklin accurate information, she became a listening post for Franklin. She brought constituent concerns to him. In her popular daily "My Day" column, which began in 1935, she refrained from political commentary except to indicate her views on public affairs by implication. Her domestic and human interest writing made the president seem more approachable and helped his image, particularly at times when he was having trouble with Congress.

Both Franklin and Eleanor were models for the nation in their enthusiasm during the days of the Depression. Eleanor's extensive travel on behalf of Franklin made it appear to the public that he traveled about with much more mobility than he was in fact able to achieve.

Eleanor continued to use various means of promoting her own public policy interest directly through persuasion of Franklin and through her contacts with other government shakers and movers. These persons would not know whether the request was Franklin's or hers, but often would not take the chance on denying what was asked.

Her reputation remained solid throughout the years of the presidency of FDR. In fact, at times when Franklin was mired in controversy, polls would show that her influence was greater than his, and there were calls for her to run for high office.

Just as Franklin drew severe criticism from time to time, so did his wife. For instance, her writing, teaching, and other interests, some for profit, were frowned upon because some persons considered these activities to commercialize the presidency and involved her, as a non-elected person, in too much political activity.

Her work to promote Arthurdale, West Virginia, as a model community for those harmed by the Depression became a subject of severe criticism toward her and the president. This West Virginia village provided by the government for displaced mine workers and others became costly and the object of scorn by those opponents charging mismanagement.

Her support of FDR's early efforts to prepare the nation for war in the late 1930's went against her basic pacifist philosophy. She finally concluded that the alternative to being ready for defending America would be worse. She also believed that the New Deal goals of support for the less fortunate and human rights should not be less important even when national security was necessary.

Having Eleanor to plead for economic and social causes was, in a way, actually beneficial to FDR. He could see how the wind was blowing before taking a position, could assess support if the idea caught on, and, sometimes, could say that an unpopular proposal was just his wife's position and not his own.

Eleanor's personality and charm proved helpful to FDR in various incidents during his long time in the presidency. For instance, the veterans of World War I had, during the presidency of Herbert Hoover, marched on Washington to urge the payment of the bonuses promised them. Hoover had sent the Army to send them home. When the vets marched again during Franklin's first term, he sent Eleanor. Without police protection, she visited the make-shift encampment, and ended up placating and even singing with the old troopers.

When the participants at the Democratic Convention of 1940 balked at nominating Henry Wallace for vice president, the choice of FDR, he called her to Chicago. She spoke to the convention and persuaded them to accept Wallace. She argued that in case her husband could not carry out his duties at any time, he needed someone capable of succeeding him. Her role was ironic in that she did not wish FDR to run for a third term in 1940 because she wished to get out of the Washington scene and felt that he had done his duty to the nation. Her opposition to the third term was also based upon her support for tradition and her fear that he would be blamed if war came. Another irony was the speculation that she might run for president the same year.

Political realities caused Eleanor to rein in long-held beliefs. The strong bloc of Southern committee chairs restrained Franklin and thus Eleanor in supporting the betterment of the conditions of African-Americans. The isolationist lobby restrained Franklin from moving forcefully for the establishment of the League of Nations and the World Court. Militants against the threat of Communism stifled legitimate concerns for the youth and other groups in international affairs. It has been said that Eleanor did not count the political cost of positions taken. This was easier for her as a non-officeholder than for Franklin. However, this refusal by Eleanor to take only safe positions operated in Franklin's favor at times, as her support for his plea for war preparedness.

All four of their sons were in military service during World War II. This and her visits to hospitals here and to military posts throughout the world heightened her advocacy of postwar peace among nations. She favored the creation of the United Nations and after Franklin's passing was appointed by President Truman as representative to that body.

Franklin showed signs of loss of strength and vitality toward the end of his third term, but Eleanor favored his running again to complete his mission in war and in the postwar period. After the fourth-term election Eleanor, even though concerned about his health, advocated a continuation of the social and economic agenda that both had supported for so long. Because of FDR's weariness, he permitted his supporters to protect him from her pleas. He sought his daughter Anna to be hostess of the White House. She and others kept his secret of continuing to be in the company of Lucy, even at the time of his passing at Warm Springs in 1945.

While Eleanor would miss Franklin very much, she continued a busy life for the next seventeen years. She was influential in politics; for example in the election of President Kennedy. Her UN post gave her the platform for an international campaign for human rights. She continued to write and lecture. Her funeral was attended by world leaders who honored her for her numerous contributions and her support in the longtime presidency of her husband. This reverence by both the powerful and the common person existed in spite of the fact that she had held no political office and had, in the main, sought anonymity in furthering both her and Franklin's agendas.

Both Franklin, 1882–1945, and Eleanor, 1884–1962, were buried in the rose garden at Hyde Park on the Hudson.

Loyalty and betrayal

Second Fiddles often contradict their Principals to their face and sometimes do things in support of Principals behind their back. These behaviors would have been normal for Eleanor and Franklin in their early years when Eleanor certainly played Second Fiddle to Franklin. They married when they were young, had an exciting social life, and had their children. They were bright and had their own opinions, so the support of Eleanor, while sound, would have come with the normal amount of questioning and doing what she felt to be good for her spouse.

What is unusual in the history of Principals and their Second Fiddles—betrayal—occurred when they were in their more mature and settled years. Franklin had from the beginning, as part of his usual exuberant behavior, the inclination toward flirting. Whether it was serious in their early years is difficult to tell, but it is known that his relationship with Lucy Mercer, as revealed to Eleanor in Lucy's letters to Franklin, caused a severity of reaction in Eleanor that would have led to separation in many marriages.

But it was the first of many such behind-the-other's-back relationships in which both of the couple engaged. Franklin may have been also intimate with Missy LeGrande, whom he traveled with and stayed with at Warm Springs, while Lucy Mercer Rutherford was part of his life until literally the very end.

Eleanor was a part of relationships with both men and women. For instance, she was very fond of Earl Miller, who was assigned to guard her and became her very good friend. She was closer than close with Lorena Hickok for thirty years or more.

Eleanor may have, as some have claimed, been basically a "man's woman" and in love with Franklin to the end. She may have taken on a "labor of love" to remain a part of his life and his career. Franklin, even though according to her secretive and failing to share his feelings, relied upon her for her moral compass and her strong positions on social justice and the well-being of the less fortunate.

So, how far did the betrayal extend? Certainly to their private lives together. Certainly to their taking up with other people. It is not, however, entirely reasonable to assume that each successfully covered up the extramarital relationships during years of very visible lives.

The mutual acts of disloyalty apparently did not extend to their partnership in public life. In so many ways Franklin relied upon her without questioning her ability, judgment, or loyalty. She nursed him through the severe case of polio and cared for his health thereafter. She took care of the family and the home in his illness and absences. She entertained and provided for their many guests and associates. She provided him with information she filtered for its truth and soundness. She gave him advice that may not have always been what he wished to hear.

She was his "legs," inspecting and investigating and reporting back, making it appear that he was very mobile when he really wasn't. She counseled him when and how to take action or refrain from action in matters of public policy. She alerted him to potential political cliffs and defused situations that might have been explosive. She defended his unpopular decisions and provided through her personality, writings, and personal contacts a balance to his attempts to cope with dangerous world, national, and political controversies.

These and other contributions she made to FDR. While they are made in close contact, they constituted their joint public response to the conditions they faced in taking on some of the most difficult issues in American public life, especially the Depression and World War II, and also running in election after election.

Second Fiddle or Principal?

Upon looking at the list of contributions of Eleanor as Second Fiddle and therefore to her obvious talents and strengths, one might ask, "Who is the Second Fiddle and who is the Principal here?" And, "How can one say that Eleanor is the Principal?"

It is not necessary to prove that she is the Principal to negate her role, especially in the White House years, as Second Fiddle. We need only to make a showing that they are equal to counter her reduced position as a Second Fiddle.

Various evidence is available to support the equality in the positions of Eleanor and her husband. The polls in the White House era showed that as Franklin had more difficulty with both the southern Democratic bloc and the Republicans in Congress in the passage of his programs, his ratings fell. Also detrimental to his standing with the public were unpopular positions he felt compelled to take for the benefit of the nation, such as the preparedness for war in the face of isolationist opposition.

Eleanor's star rose at times when Franklin's fell. Her positive and warm personality shone through in her personal contacts and her radio and other media activities. She was in the background and not in the forefront of advocacy, and she could operate behind the scenes more easily than Franklin. Her appeal was such that the public and political pundits and personages touted her for the highest offices in the land.

She, of course, incurred wrath against her person and her ideas. Cruel comments were made about her physical appearance, her dress, and her high speaking voice. She was lambasted for her liberalism and her commercialization of the presidency by accepting fees for writing and speaking. Programs she advocated that did not live up to expectations, such as the Arthurdale housing project, did not escape the notice of critics.

The main reason for the argument that Eleanor maintained sufficient equality with Franklin to counter her position as Second Fiddle and his being the sole Principal was the agenda she set and pushed and accomplished while he was in positions of power. Even though she held no elected office, she was able to further a social agenda that included improvement in the rights of minorities, women, and children; employment; a full draft rather than permitting escape from serving in the armed forces; and world peace issues, including advocacy for the League of Nations, the World Court, and the United Nations. Not all of her agenda was accomplished, but enough that one may conclude that during much of her life she was not a Second Fiddle.

And all of this without appearing to have power, of being anonymous in an era when women had still not received much independence, and should still be "kept in their place." She did it with care, seeming to go through Franklin, with his permission, and with the intent, at least, of not angering him. She said that women in politics must have "the wisdom of the serpent and the guileless appearance of the dove." It is true, however, that in the last part of his life, he grew weary and less amenable to her suggestions, to the point of avoiding her with the help of staff and, sometimes, members of the family.

Perhaps we may conjecture further, based on the evidence of her contributions, that she was at least in some ways and in some periods of their marriage, the Principal to Franklin's Second Fiddle. One might explore whether FDR and Eleanor were playing a game that took place on two levels—one as a couple, and one in the pursuit of politics and public policy.

Various tests might be applied to the life of independence and dependence of this remarkable couple, but looking at them from the standpoint of Principal and Second Fiddle, it is by no means clear that he was the former and she the latter.

2

Watson and Holmes

Among the best-known enduring relationships in fiction is that of Sherlock Holmes as leader and John Watson as follower. Most of the followers of the detective and his companion would agree with Christopher Morley's preface to *The Complete Sherlock Holmes*: "We must begin in Baker Street; and best of all, if possible, let it be a stormy winter morning when Holmes routs Watson out of bed in haste. The doctor wakes to see that tall ascetic figure by the bedside with a candle. 'Come, Watson, come! The game is afoot.'"

This well-known scene tells us a bit about which of the two men has greater influence in their relationship. From film and television as well as from selected events in the cases emerges a fairly simple popular notion of Holmes and Watson as they relate to each other. That notion is one of Holmes, the Principal, and Watson, the Second Fiddle; Holmes critical of his associate, and Watson failing in his accomplishment of assignments given him.

A more complex view of the relationship emerges from a fair sampling of the books and stories written by Arthur Conan Doyle about the detective and his friend, Watson. Their adventures together contradict the popular impression of these individuals. Of course, a pattern at the base of the stories is Holmes' trusting reliance on Watson and the latter's support and admiration for the detective. Other patterns of mutuality emerge, however, from a closer look at the writings. In counterpoint to the positive nature of the friendship is criticism from time to time by both men of each other. In addition to the evident concern shown by each are disagreements and shows of independence by the two. And, the evident strengths of the often-maligned Watson emerge time and time again.

Watson's abilities

The apex of trust and reliance is expressed by Holmes in "A Scandal in Bohemia" when Holmes urges Watson to stay on at 221B Baker street, saying that "I am lost without my Boswell." This, of course, is a reference to the biographer and associate of Dr. Samuel Johnson, James Boswell. It presumably refers not only to Watson as recorder of the feats of the detective but also to the association between the two.

And why shouldn't Holmes find Watson capable of providing great assistance? When they met, Watson was a trained medical doctor and had served in the Army as a combat surgeon. During their long association the Doctor established and maintained a medical practice. Because of this training and experience, he was able to provide reliable medical and scientific advice. For instance, in "A Study in Scarlet" Jefferson Hope was apprehended by Holmes for committing the murder of two men. Before telling why he did it, involving the terrible treatment the men had perpetrated on the woman he wished to marry, Hope permitted Dr. Watson to examine him for a medical problem. The Doctor detected an aortic aneurysm which was threatening the life of the murderer.

On occasion Watson was called upon to use his healing talents on behalf of his friend. In one instance this valuable service was offered even when not wanted. In "The Adventures of the Dying Detective," Holmes' long-time landlady, Mrs. Hudson, called on Dr. Watson in a frantic plea to come to Baker Street. She feared that Holmes was near death from some disease he was investigating. Watson came to the apartment at once and saw Holmes' dire condition, but his friend would not let him come near, saying that he had a disease that required the Doctor to keep his distance.

Watson replied that disease would not prevent him from helping a stranger, and that it would not prevent him from "doing my duty to so old a friend." Holmes then belittled Watson's abilities, saying he was "only a general practitioner with very limited experience and mediocre qualifications." Instead he asked the Doctor to summon an expert in far Eastern diseases.

Watson eventually learns that Holmes has been faking his condition for purposes of resolving the mystery. At the successful conclusion of the matter with Watson's help, Holmes asks him, "Do you imagine that I have no respect for your medical talents?'

Discretion was another valuable trait of Watson. Visitors to 221B Baker Street were time and again assured that they could speak in front of the Doctor as freely as with Holmes. Watson seldom interrupted Holmes' interrogation of clients; however, the Doctor's presence permits him to hear all the facts from the beginning so as to be more helpful in rendering useful opinions.

Holmes' trust and reliance

Watson served consistently as a sounding board for Holmes. In "The Adventure of the Blanched Soldier" written by Holmes himself, he took the occasion to admit that he missed Watson's "cunning questions" and expressions of wonder that elevated Holmes' "common sense" conclusions "into a prodigy."

Watson was called upon to give real physical assistance in "The Adventure of Black Peter," when the two men were conducting surveillance at the house of some subjects of the investigation. In order to see over a wall Holmes asked Watson to permit him to stand on the Doctor's shoulders.

Watson was sometimes assigned tasks in which he would work independently of Holmes. When the detective was occupied, he would send Watson to make a useful contact or to investigate, return, and report. For instance, Watson traveled on one occasion to Surrey and another time to Switzerland.

Watson is occasionally drawn in when Holmes feels the need to take the law into his own hands while investigating a case. In "A Scandal in Bohemia," Holmes immediately sees through the disguise of a visitor who turns out to be the King of Bohemia. The King has had an affair with Irene Adler, a famous opera singer, and is being blackmailed by her. The basis for the blackmail is a picture he had taken with her during the affair. Incidentally, Madame Adler is known in Sherlockian circles as "The Woman," and, some say, the only woman Holmes ever loved.

After proceeding, in disguise, to observe the woman's house, the detective devises a scheme to locate the photo and separate it from its owner. The plan involves Watson's participation. After explaining the case to the Doctor, Holmes inquires whether Watson minds breaking the laws. Watson agrees to help by throwing a smoke bomb into a window. This action aided in their solving the mystery, but it would not have been appreciated by the police of the day.

Late in their mutual career in "The Case of Charles Augustus Milverton," they discuss the justifiability of Holmes' entering a home and committing burglary. Watson believes that this crime is to be perpetrated if only illegal items are removed. When Holmes tries to exclude Watson from the caper, Watson asserts that he will either be permitted to go along or he will go to the police. They, as usual, enter the house and bring the case to a conclusion.

The highest form of dependence by Holmes upon his friend would, of course, be his asking Watson to take some action involving life and death, or, at least, concerning a dangerous situation. On a number of occasions Holmes inquires of Watson whether he is armed. Watson obliges by employing a variety of weapons on numerous occasions.

The use of the weapons goes beyond a simple show of force. In "The Red-headed League" a pawn broker with a "blazing red head" won a contest with other similarly coifed men. As a prize he was awarded a stipend each week in return for his copying from the *Encyclopedia Britannica.* The copying was to be performed in an office in another part of town. He sought out Holmes when that office closed abruptly, and he became suspicious of the persons who had held the contest.

As the mystery progresses and the two friends are sitting in a dark cellar waiting for "daring men" bent on robbery, Holmes positions himself and Watson behind crates as shields. Then Holmes gives the order, "when I flash a light upon them, close in swiftly. If they fire, Watson, have no compunction about shooting them down." As a result of the element of surprise and swift action by Holmes in disarming the leader by the use of a hunting crop, there was no need to use firearms. It was a real possibility, however, in this and other times in the sleuthing endeavors.

Among other weapons they relied upon Watson's walking stick more than once.

And, after a threat by a visitor to their lodgings had subsided in "The Adventure of the Three Gables" later in their career, Holmes off-handily said that he had observed Watson's "manoeuvres with the poker."

Companionship

Sherlock Holmes has had through the years a reputation for self-reliance, confidence to the point of haughtiness, and a clinical level of keeping personal feelings out of his work in solving mysteries. In light of this well-known persona his reliance upon and appreciation of Watson for his companionship may be surprising. Even when Watson acknowledged in "A Scandal in Bohemia" that Holmes was "not effusive," Watson thought Holmes was glad to see him.

Other indications of Holmes' appreciation of his friend's company were more direct. In "The Adventure of the Norwood Builder" when the two were living separately, Holmes suggested that Watson sell his practice and move back into 221B. Another instance occurred when Watson thought Holmes to have died as a result of his plunge over the Reichenbach Falls.

Watson had recorded in "The Final Problem" the terrible shock he had received upon his visit to the fall of Reichenbach. He saw there the evidence of Holmes' struggle with his arch-enemy, Professor Moriarty, and his plunge over the cliff to his death.

Three years later, 1894, in "The Adventure of the Empty House," missing his friend, the Doctor followed the case of the death of a young man, Ronald Adair, who had been shot and killed in a locked room. Considering this to be a case that would have interested Holmes, Watson visited the home where Adair had been killed, and there bumped into an old, deformed book peddler.

When Watson returned home, the book peddler visited him, and to Watson's shock so severe that he passed out, Sherlock Holmes emerged from the disguise of his visitor's pathetic form.

"'My dear Watson,' said the well-remembered voice, 'I owe you a thousand apologies. I had no idea that you would be so affected.'" Then Holmes went on to say that their meeting again was "like the old days."

"Dr. Watson and I are at your service," says Holmes in "The Adventure of the Three Gables." In addition to the mutual support in times of danger and in the solving of difficult issues, the two colleagues experienced numerous lesser contacts that gave evident of their lasting friendship. On occasion they would share a laugh or take "evening rambles." During an exceptionally tense moment in "His Last Bow" Holmes gives his partner's hand a "reassuring shake," after which they ran two miles in order to elude pursuers.

In that same adventure just before World War I, Holmes, long retired, is visited by Watson. He says the well-known lines that sums up their time together: "Stand with me on the terrace." He indicates that this may be the old friends' "last quiet talk we shall ever have."

In addition to these "quiet" contacts, appellations by which Holmes refers to Watson are revealing of the relationship of Principal and Second Fiddle. At various times

Watson is called Holmes' representative, comrade, partner, helper, old friend, and biographer. And, at the time of the uncertainty of the approach of World War I, Watson is "the one fixed point in a changing age."

The long litany of support and praise by Watson is not matched by Holmes; however, some moments in their long association are instructive as to the detective's close notice of his friend. Over and over Holmes "reads" the Doctor's thoughts and then reveals the steps that lead him to what Watson is thinking. In their first case together Holmes asks whether Watson's leg which was injured in war would stand a long hike. And, on a lighter note, Holmes on one occasion sought Watson's approval of his abilities as a cook.

Watson's support and praise

Not only did Watson render valuable assistance in various ways, he did it willingly and often enthusiastically. "I'm here to be used, Holmes," he said in "The Adventure of the Illustrious Client," in response to Holmes' request for assistance. Passing 221B when he had other living quarters, he said he was "keen" to see Holmes again. He felt "joy" upon seeing his friend whom he thought had perished over the falls of Reichenbach. In "His Last Bow" he said that he feels twenty years younger and is seldom as happy as when he received a request by Holmes to meet him.

Even in times of danger he readily agrees to help. In "The Adventure of the Illustrious Client" he offers to "thrash the hide off" an attacker. When Holmes considers himself about to be murdered in "The Adventure of the Mazarin Stone," Watson wants to come to his aid, even though neither is any longer young. Holmes recognizes his friend's sincerity: "You have never failed to play the game. I am sure you will play it to the end."

Watson is unstinting in his praise of Holmes throughout their career. The Doctor is amazed at the way in which his Principal solves case after case. He lauds Holmes' "incisive reasoning," and exhibits extreme faith in Holmes' abilities.

Watson's offer early in their association to publish Holmes' success in solving cases was, of course, a form of praise and flattery. Watson continued to record the detective's successes even though Holmes at times was critical of the manner in which some adventures were presented. When Holmes takes on the responsibility of writer in addition to problem solver, he has to admit that the task is not as easy as he had believed.

During the period when Watson thought Holmes to be deceased, he employed Holmes' methods for his "private satisfaction." Imitation provided a clue as to the extreme confidence he had in the sleuth's capabilities.

The closeness of association provides the opportunity of the two friends to observe each other's mannerisms. In "The Adventure of the Solitary Cyclist" Watson reveals that he sees sides of Holmes to which others are not privy. He sees his colleague both profoundly excited and very despondent.

Criticism, disagreements, and independence

No close association is a perpetual mutual admiration performance, and this is true of our subjects here. Holmes, of course, is the more critical of the two. His lack of respect for Watson's intellect was especially evident in their early days together. In "A Study in Scarlet" Holmes showed his frustration with his companion by not expecting Watson to understand a part of the puzzle before them. Later in the same adventure, when Watson did not grasp an essential element, Holmes went so far as to say, "You surprise me." On numerous occasions, not only does he assume Watson will be in the dark as to the importance and interpretation of the clues that they both observe, but he is very direct in pointing out shortcomings of his associate.

These shortcomings include Watson's poor performance of tasks assigned him.

In "The Disappearance of Lady Frances Carfax" Holmes chides Watson, "I cannot at the moment recall any possible blunder which you have omitted. The total effect of your proceeding has been to give the alarm everywhere and yet to discover nothing."

In "The Adventure of the Solitary Cyclist" a young woman, Violet Smith, has been hired to teach piano to a child whose home is in Surrey. She rides her bicycle on a lonely stretch of country road on the way to and from the railway station on her visits home to London. She is followed time and again, at a distance, by a male cyclist.

When she consults with Sherlock Holmes regarding this strange happening, he assigns Watson to go to Surrey to observe secretly the man following her. Upon Watson's return Holmes "austere face was even more severe" as he criticized Watson for choosing a hiding place for observation that was too far away to permit him to get a good look at the cyclist. Holmes concludes that Watson has done "remarkably badly." Further, Watson had failed to obtain information about the suspicious inhabitants of an estate near where Violet saw the solitary cyclist. Holmes says that, instead of going to a real estate agent for information,

Watson should have gone to "the nearest public house. That is the center of country gossip."

Watson's marriage was the subject of Holmes' concern on more than one occasion. He held that Watson had deserted him for a wife, the doctor's only "selfish action." Further, he "feared" the marriage because of its effect of impairing the Doctor's reason.

Watson readily admits to being in the dark as to Holmes' procedure for solving crimes. In "The Red-headed League" he admits a "sense of his own stupidity" in dealing with his friend who has "keener senses" than he has.

Watson, in defense, points out in "The Adventure of the Empty House" that Holmes shows "temper" and impatience with those with less intelligence than his. Watson also records his opinion of Holmes' "egotism and vanity."

Usually, however, the doctor's critical comments are lighter. For instance, when the two old friends meet in later life on the South Downs where Holmes has been bee-keeping, Watson notes that he has changed little, except for his "horrible goatee." When Watson is smitten by Mary Morestan, who becomes his wife, he suggests in "A Study in Scarlet" that the detective has "inhuman qualities" in not noticing her beauty.

This lack of notice on the part of Holmes may relate to one of several disagreements between the two friends. Holmes contends that women cannot be trusted, while Watson takes the opposite view. Another point which they debate is whether life and truth are "more daring" or stranger than fiction, with Holmes on the affirmative and Watson on the negative.

While the two friends form one of the closest bonds in fiction, each has ways of maintaining his independence.

Holmes has his solitary ways that involve experiments, cogitation, cocaine, his pipe and violin, and periodic absences from their quarters. On rare occasions he cannot confide in his biographer in particularly sensitive cases.

Watson marries and leaves their lodgings at 221B, during which time he doesn't see Holmes as much. And, he has a medical practice which commands his time and energies.

What can be said of the relationship of Watson and Holmes?

At first glance and, as usually portrayed, Holmes is a critical taskmaster, for whom Watson can do nothing right. Watson himself confesses that he is in awe of Holmes' abilities, and that he considers himself to be lacking in intellect. Some of this relates to Sir Arthur Conan Doyle's calling him "Holmes' rather stupid friend," and some from the portrayal of the Doctor in early plays and films.

A closer look at the association of the apparent Principal, Holmes, and the evident Second Fiddle, Watson, indicates that the relationship is more complex than adherents of the two friends might assume. Extensive evidence of their critical outlook toward each other exists in the writings, but extreme reliance, even to the point of life and death, is found frequently.

Holmes does criticize Watson for failures in carrying out assignments, but compliments the Doctor for his medical expertise and other forms of assistance. Watson is anything but a bumbler when called upon to render medical opinion or treatment. And Watson includes in his reporting of the cases a variety of complaints about Holmes' traits of temper, egotism, and vanity.

In addition to being a complex relationship, their association can be seen as an evolving one. The progression from sharing rooms simply as a monetary matter transcends into one of significant mutual trust, and, although difficult given the personality of Holmes, of mutual affection. The overwhelming majority of actions and statements by Dr. Watson were based on an unyielding loyalty. Otherwise, why would this correct English Doctor and gentleman engage in criminal activity, such as breaking and entering in order to obtain clues, or engage in gunfire to protect his friend. And, it is recorded that he even takes risks solely on Holmes' request, not knowing all of the implications of the actions taken.

How uncharacteristic of Holmes, as initially seen at 221B Baker Street, to refer to the Doctor later on as "good old Watson" and "a trusted companion." When Watson was shot in "The Three Garridebs," Holmes cried "You're not hurt, Watson? For God's sake, say that you are not hurt."

Two final questions remain. First, what motivates Watson to be the Second Fiddle to Holmes? Certainly friendship leads to the desire to assist and to protect Holmes, who disregards his own safety and health. But, even more than that affinity between the two, Watson enjoys the diversions that the mysteries bring. He says the adventures make him feel "useful" and "younger." Finally, Watson may enjoy his role of recorder of the exploits of the world's first consulting detective.

A second question involves the ways in which the Principal here is enhanced by the Second Fiddle. Certainly, a strong, competent associate is useful in solving the detective's cases. The Doctor is there to render medical aid to persons involved in the mysteries as well as to Holmes himself. Watson's steady personality balances Holmes' impetuosity. Holmes owes his survival on occasion to his friend's protective actions. And, in spite of his protestation, Holmes presumably actually enjoyed the notoriety he experienced from Watson's "stories."

All the complexities of the relationship and the long evolution from strangers to companions underscore the lengthy friendship between these two men. The opportunity for analysis abounds as to the reasons for their close companionship over many years. In spite of this, overemphasis or too-lengthy analysis of their association falls by the wayside, as it should, when we simply take up the mysteries in hand and read, as in "The Adventure of the Abbey Grange," as Holmes cries, "Come, Watson, come! The game is afoot."

3

Max Perkins and
Ernest Hemingway

A Second Fiddle supports the leader, the Principal, and stays in the background. When we think of the typical person who fills the role of the Second Fiddle, we are usually thinking of one individual. But what if the Second Fiddle develops and furthers the success of a number of individuals? A coach might do just that. This would not apply to the prominent university basketball coach who is as much in the public eye as their best known player; rather, the school soccer coach who works on the skills of players but stays in the background, or the voice or drama coach, or the art instructor.

The book editor who seeks out and develops numerous writers might be added to this list. One such editor, preeminent among his peers in the nineteen twenties through forties, was Max Perkins. His career in shaping some of our finest authors will be instructive in determining whether one who supports numerous others may be considered a Second Fiddle.

First we will look closely at what an editor does. We will accomplish this through Max Perkins' relationship with four of his writers. These writers were F. Scott Fitzgerald, Thomas Wolfe, Ernest Hemingway, and James Jones. It will be seen that each relationship varied from the others. For instance, it was a constant need of making money arrangements for Fitzgerald, while hard, intense work was required to bring together in coherent fashion the vast array of pages generated by Wolfe. Similarities among the needs of the writers will also be evident in the examples. Each of the examples will be followed by comments.

After these editor-author illustrations the life story of Max Perkins will be given to show how his background influenced the effectiveness of the support that he could bring to bear upon the careers of the illustrated writers. This biography of Perkins will be followed by conclusions as to whether one person may be a Second Fiddle to many Principals.

F. Scott Fitzgerald

In the fall of 1924 F. Scott Fitzgerald sent to his editor, Max Perkins, the manuscript of a novel, *Among the Ash Heaps and Millionaires*, that Fitzgerald considered the best American novel ever written. Ever striving for perfection he had been his own best editor until the point of turning the manuscript over to Perkins, the "go to" editor for young writers. Scott was 27.

He had been going through a bad time, with excessive drinking, living beyond his means with his wife, Zelda, despondent, and in debt. He had not written a novel in a while and considered himself to be lazy. He had been moving from place to place with his wife Zelda, enjoying a life style well beyond his means. He was living on Long Island when he received the letter from his editor, Maxfield Perkins of Scribner's, in which Perkins suggested that he have a novel, his third, to be ready for the spring list. As was his way, Perkins gave encouragement and told Scott to proceed at his own pace.

As a result of this encouragement, Scott was strengthened to the point of turning out the novel and awaited Perkins' assessment no matter how good or how bad. Perkins responded that he thought the novel splendid, a wonder, and that it captured the life of the times. He gave lavish, sincere praise as to the quality of the work, but at the same time made suggestions for changes. For instance, Perkins felt that the title needed to be changed. After reviewing numerous possibilities, author and editor agreed on *The Great Gatsby*.

Perkins suggested several structural changes. For instance, he noted that the sources of Gatsby's wealth had not been explained. Possible remedies might include phone calls with unknown persons and discussions at parties with mysterious individuals. Perkins suggested that, rather than accumulating in one place the description of Gatsby's past, this information should be inserted here and there throughout the book.

Mixed with the suggestions were further words of high praise for the characters of Tom, Daisy, and Jordan and for other features of the novel. Evidently the joining of praise with criticism was effective because Scott's reaction was that Max's words made him more confident to make nearly all the suggested changes. As an example he introduced conversations that revealed more of Gatsby's past, and let the reader know that Gatsby had partnered with another in buying a Chicago drugstore for the purpose of the sale of bootleg alcohol.

During these exchanges Fitzgerald, who was ever in need of money and typically in debt to Scribner's, and sometimes even to Perkins personally, requested a sum of money toward the advance on the book. As a means of repaying Scribner's he requested a reduction on the percentage of his royalty. There ensued an odd negotiation in which Perkins was arguing for holding the line on the royalty. Finally, they agree to a percentage in the middle.

The sales of *The Great Gatsby* were very disappointing, to the degree that Fitzgerald was in despair because he felt he would continue to need money and could not reduce his high lifestyle. He considered stopping the writing of novels and perhaps going to work in the motion picture industry in Hollywood.

The reviews were generally very good even if not up to Max's high praise to Scott of the merits of the novel. Max believed that some of the negative reviewers as well as the public had missed Scott's satirical approach to the party life on Long Island. He continued to buoy up Scott with positive words.

A rumor circulated that Scott was considering leaving Scribners for another publisher. Scott denied this, giving various reasons, including the fair and generous dealings that he had experienced from Max and Mr. Scribner. Scott also likely noted that Max typically was as enthusiastic about his authors' writings as they were themselves.

(The preceding includes a summary of events leading to the publication of *The Great Gatsby,* from A. Scott Berg's *Max Perkins: Editor of Genius* (New York: New American Library, 1978), pp. 49, 60–86. Berg describes a premier editor in his development of some of the major writers of his day. Berg makes extensive use of primary sources, including letters among the parties.)

The description of Perkins' work with Fitzgerald in the development of this book reveals or at least hints at some of the variety of roles of an editor. Some of these roles are very predictable, but some outside the editor's usual job description. Of course editors edit. They read and suggest revisions designed to improve characters, plot, setting, and action. They determine how much to push the writer so that they will be willing to take on the task of the various requests. They arrange the contractual arrangements, including advances and royalties for the project. They arrange for the design, printing, and publication of the product.

This interchange with Scott Fitzgerald sheds light on more than the traditional work of the editor. Even if one would admit the extreme of the insecurity of the young Fitzgerald and the questionable choices he and his wife Zelda were making, the acts of praise and caring exhibited by Perkins illuminate the supportive, empathetic role of the editor. Perhaps Max goes even further than most in his patience and forbearance with Scott and various other authors of his day, especially considering Max's emphasis on the development of young authors who represented the age in which they were living.

In dealing with young authors who were often without independent means, dealings between Max and Scott show an extreme case of chronic need of money. Max throughout his career went further than most editors in coming up with creative solutions. For instance, in addition to securing loans by Scribners, Max made personal loans and arranged for the publication of Scott's stories in his publisher's magazine. Scott often fretted about his debt to the company and payed it back as he could. Other examples of Max's financial services were arranging for an anthology by Ring Lardner, a Guggenheim Fellowship for

Thomas Wolfe, and the management of various writer's funds.

Thomas Wolfe

After the publication of *Look Homeward, Angel*, Thomas Wolfe began writing furiously about his own life. The extent of his writings would fill ten novels, and he added some 50,000 words a month. His editor, Max Perkins, began to fret about the effect of the work on Wolfe's health, that perhaps he was headed for a breakdown. Perkins took the drastic step of telling Tom that he had done enough on his new novel, and that it was time to stop.

Tom reluctantly agreed and in the winter of 1933 delivered a bundle of manuscript two feet high to his editor. It was out of order and in disarray, and he needed editorial help in bringing it together. Max was convinced that Wolfe was a genius, but that he needed to be bolstered in his belief in himself and needed emotional support. So Editor Max took on the most extensive task of his life.

Just before Christmas Wolfe delivered the rest of the work, making a total of a million words. In sorting it all out, writer and editor determined to divide the writing into two novels, *Of Time and the River*, to which they gave their immediate attention, and *The October Fair.*

In the beginning writer and editor worked every day for two hours in the spring of 1934. Soon they began working nights beginning at 8:30, Monday through Saturday. Then they added Sunday to their schedule as they proceeded through the heat of summer in New York City. Jokes began to circulate about their extreme schedule.

A major part of the effort was in cutting words through eliminating or reducing scenes. Some of the scenes extended

50,000 to 80,000 words. Max and Tom argued over every cut, with Tom finally agreeing nearly all of the time. On one scene Max suggested that the thirty thousand words tended to take away a certain amount of the suspense that Tom desired. Another part of the effort was adding dialogue and filling in gaps. The difficulty was that where Tom needed only a few words he would get carried away in his writing and that, too, had to be edited downward. In spite of the degree of contention between the two men, Wolfe declared that his editor had brought the project to conclusion through strength and determination.

Of Time and the River was a great success both artistically and commercially. The reviews were generally enthusiastic and publication required several printings. However, Tom who had gone to Europe, fretted about the errors in spelling and consistency in the story, feeling that more time should have been taken. He even accused Max of interfering with the quality of the product. Max denied this and sought to counter Tom's concerns, ever wishing to support and protect his writers, often from themselves. In any event Wolfe had successfully completed the hurdle of a second novel and hoped to be able to alleviate the frantic activity that his writing had become. Wolfe enjoyed the adoration of his fans, indicated by the fact that he received more mail at Scribner's than any other of their writers.

As seen from this editor-writer description from Berg, pp. 234–270, the amount of work by both editor and author in the production of this very successful novel was certainly extreme. It indicates that an editor is engaged in a very labor-intensive activity that goes well beyond what might be expected. Max's efforts to protect the writer from himself in his overwork and expectations and from the effects of the criticism of others is instructive as to another role of the editor. Also, the decision to stop Wolfe's writing and start preparing the manuscript for publication indicates the need for the editor at times to make difficult and dramatic decisions.

Ernest Hemingway

In the fall of 1939 as the war in Europe was getting underway, Ernest Hemingway was writing his novel that was based upon his first-hand experiences the Spanish Civil War. He had plans to engage in some way in the new war but was holding off until the novel was completed. He was doing his writing at a ranch in Montana, but soon moved to a suite in a resort in Sun Valley, Idaho.

He had completed 90,000 words which his editor, Max Perkins, hoped to publish in the Scribner's spring list. The party atmosphere in Sun Valley took over, however, and Hemingway joined in. The result was a break until he moved to a villa in Cuba. In response to Max's pleas he sent pages of the new novel. Max was pleased with the sample and sent Hemingway a contract. Work on the novel resumed, partially due to the arrival of Martha Gellhorn, a younger, very attractive novelist, who was more than just a friend.

Hemingway wanted a title to match the bigness of the volume he was preparing. Of some thirty titles he considered he chose *For Whom the Bell Tolls*. Max thought the choice appropriate for what he considered an excellent book. He was relieved to have Ernest finally completing his first novel in ten years. In July Hemingway wired Max "Bridge all blown": The novel was competed.

Hemingway came to New York where he spent the month of August and into September with Max. Max suggested changes with Ernest at his side in the office. Most of the changes dealt with details; however, some were more important and led to arguments between writer and editor. Ernest agreed to some, but at others he balked, claiming that the way the matter was expressed fit the story. For instance, he had written that an old woman had forecast a "smell of death to come." Max considered the language too strong, but Ernest claimed it to be suitable for publication, and it was kept. Hemingway had opted for an epilogue, which Max considered to take away from Hemingway's conclusion of the novel. Ernest agreed to drop the epilogue.

As befitting what Max believed to be a great book Scribner's went all out in presenting the book to the public. The Christmas window at the Scribner's book store was totally devoted to a display of the novel. The result of this publicity campaign and the critical acclaim the book received resulted in huge sales. The Book-of-the-Month Club adoption alone amounted to a quarter of a million.

In the midst of this effort to bring out Hemingway's novel, in December, 1939, F. Scott Fitzgerald passed away. In addition to the shock of the death of such a close associate over the years, Max had to assume extensive duties in regard to Scott's estate and literary contributions. As a result Max could not devote the time needed to keep Ernest Hemingway informed of progress in the sales of his book.

In the spring Hemingway had gone off to war again, this time to Hong Kong to cover the Sino-Japanese War. He felt that Max was neglecting his interest in favor of Fitzgerald's estate, saying that several ships had arrived in Hong Kong with no word from Max. In an effort to make amends Max wrote successive letters to Hemingway about the progress of his novel. One of the important pieces of news was the sales had reached nearly half a million copies.

This episode in the editing of an important book (from Berg, pp. 375–396) by Ernest Hemingway gives further illumination of the various roles performed by an editor. Dealing with a person so full of life as Hemingway was not easy. Just keeping up with him as he moved from place to place, and keeping up with the movements of any author is important because of the need of contact at various stages of the production of a work, from idea, inception through editing and publication.

Even if it is a particularly unproductive period, getting the attention of the author for the presentation of ideas and keeping on schedule is important. Partying and alcohol have a way of being very distracting to individuals, keeping them from coming up with a manuscript, as in the above case with the ten-year hiatus of Hemingway between books.

Publicity is an important part of bringing out a writing. Of course, it helps to have a good novel or other work, but the ability of the editor and the publishing house to go full-tilt in getting the public to want to buy is vital. The author, who has invested so much of themselves in the product, is bound to be concerned if it looks as if little effort is being made to sell the book. Then, too, as with Ernest Hemingway, one may become concerned that other authors' interests, in this case, Fitzgerald's, are taking precedence.

James Jones

James Jones served with the Army Air Corps in Hawaii before and during the Second World War. There he discovered his interest in writing, and especially emulated Thomas Wolfe, whose upbringing seemed to be similar to Jones'. He sent his first novel to Max Perkins, who was in the latter stage of his career and was a legend among young writers. Perkins discussed the novel, *They Shall Inherit the Laughter,* with the twenty-four-year-old Jones and rejected it for publication, but not before noting that Jones appeared to have what it takes to make a successful writer.

Jones revised his novel and wrote that he was anxious to get on with various writing ideas including a second novel, about class distinctions among enlisted men and higher ranks in the Army prior to World War II. Max was very much interested in this idea and offered a $500 option on the unwritten work.

Jones pledged to follow Max's instructions even though he did not like to give up on his first novel. Jones respected the editor's experience and reputation and went to work. At the same time Max was anxious to get this new novel, as he wished to help guide the new generation of writers who were coming out of the wartime period. Max saw changes coming and wanted to be ahead of these changes.

Writer and editor met on several occasions, and Max gave various suggestions. One was that the writer should stop when doing well and not wait until they were having difficulty with the writing. Max also indicated that the successful writer was one who sensed acutely their writing environment at the time they were producing their product. Success was more than just writing for remuneration.

Late in 1946 Jones sent a number of pages of *From Here to Eternity* to Perkins. At this stage Jones considered Perkins to be a father figure, almost to the extent of Thomas Wolfe's relationship with Max. In spring, 1947,

Max advised Jones that the writer should not become so involved with plot that he would abandon a flexibility in seeking new creative avenues.

Unfortunately, by this time in the association with the young author, Max Perkins had become very infirm and was approaching the end of his life. Communication between the revered editor and James Jones came to an end and Max Perkins passed on in June, 1947.

James Jones' relationship with Max Perkins, as found in Berg, pp. 433–37, and 447–48, came to be based upon complete reliance and trust, even to the extent of Perkins assuming a level of substitute parenthood. Jones was aware of the reputation of Perkins as the developer of new writers, and became more dependent as their association progressed. Even facing disappointment in the rejection of his first novel, Jones managed to move ahead with renewed confidence in the production of *From Here to Eternity* on the faith in his editor.

It is ironic that at the time of failing health Max Perkins was looking forward to the new generation of postwar writers. He wished to help develop the best of the lot, including James Jones, who would set high writing standards for the new generation. He had been performing this service to the world of publishing since just after the previous world war.

Max Perkins

Although born in Manhattan on September 10, 1884, William Maxwell Evarts Perkins always thought of himself as New England bred, and, in fact, settled himself in summers there, in Vermont, as a relief from the oppression of the City. His family heritage, extending in this country back to the seventeenth century on both sides, was a combining of the Evarts family with Perkins. According to Berg's description of his life, largely in Chapter III, "Provenance," the Evarts were more dedicated to hard work and a serious approach to life while the Perkins leaned more toward the enjoyment of a freer and more artistic lifestyle. Max reflected this dichotomy in his choice of economics as a Harvard course of study while heavily engaging in the pursuit of literature, and in his exhausting schedule of editing work while encouraging the progress of new generations of authors.

His father had died when Max was eighteen, leaving his family less well off than many of his peers. His first job out of college was teaching English to immigrants in Boston, followed by employment by the *New York Times* as a police reporter.

He had known future wife, Elizabeth Saunders, of Plainfield, New Jersey, since their childhood. He married Elizabeth of December 31, 1910. She had always desired to be an actress. The next years were spent in raising a family of five children, all daughters. Max was very close with the girls, especially enjoying reading to them from a variety of authors.

1910 was also the year that Perkins was hired by Scribners, a well-established rather conservative New York publishing house. His first position was that of advertising manager, but he was added to the editorial staff in 1914. He became one of the leading figures at Scribners, and was made Editor-in-Chief and vice president in 1932. His tenure at the publishing house lasted from 1910 to his death on June 17, 1947.

During Max Perkins' years of editing he developed many of the leading writers of his era. In addition to Fitzgerald,

Wolfe, Hemingway, and James Jones, he had edited Ring Lardner, and John P. Marquand, S.S. VanDyne, Alan Paton, Will James, and Alice Roosevelt Longworth. Among numerous others were Marjorie Kinnan Rawlings, Arthur Train, Bruce Barton, and Erskine Caldwell. Max was the favored destination of a young writer seeking to become an established author.

The describing of his relationship with Fitzgerald, Wolfe, Hemingway, and James Jones is meant to give insight into Perkins' working with a variety of important writers at various stages of their careers and during the progression of Max's influence upon American letters. All of this occurred while Max held to the belief that the editor should be in the background while the public is permitted to see only the writer, and only at their best.

Perkins: A Second Fiddle?

Through the relationships of Max Perkins with four of his most prominent writers we have seen how editors go about molding their authors to a high degree of proficiency and marketability. The editor performs numerous roles in addition to editing. These roles include the recognition and search for promising individuals, providing not only financial but also psychological support, dealing with spouses and others surrounding the writers, and other tasks that one would not imagine that an editor would have to assume.

Editors are a product of their backgrounds, and this can be seen in the life of Max Perkins. In his work with the authors in the examples given we can see his love of literature, his penchant for hard, intense work, and his desire to remain out of the limelight.

Similarities can be seen between the contributions of the Second Fiddle who support one Principal and the Second Fiddle who works to develop numerous individuals. This is especially true in the affective realm, where the empathetic ear may be as significant as the performance of the technical task. The Second Fiddle may be as apt to be called upon to promote or protect a single Principal as numerous ones. Remaining in the background was as much a characteristic of Editor Max Perkins as would be the case of the executive assistant of a captain of industry.

Of course, the obvious difference with the example of the editor is in the numerous rather than the single Principal. The Second Fiddle to a single Principal is most often an assistant rather than an instructor. Instructing in this situation could be detrimental to the relationship if not done with tact. The editor as well as the coach or instructor, provide their instruction in intense but sporadic doses, while the Second Fiddle who is an assistant most often performs tasks continuously day-to-day. Of editing it has been said that much of the time a person of lesser skills could do the job, but at other times it is necessary for the editor to bring all his talents of guiding writing and matters of quality and taste, as well as forbearance.

We may conclude from looking at Editor Perkins and his authors and comparing those relationships with the Second Fiddle and single Principal that the similarities outweigh the differences, as distinct as the differences are. The presence of multiple Principals does not appear to get in the way of the essentials of supporting others and remaining in the background.

If this conclusion is valid, it reveals an entirely new dimension for the study of the relationship between Second

Fiddle and Principal(s). This dimension would include those coaches of sport, the arts, and other skills, who remain in the background and let the light shine on those whose lives and careers they promote. This may lead to the study of other Second Fiddle and multiple-Principal relationships.

A final question is necessary: Is the editor in some ways a Principal? In editing they have a major hand in determining the length, characteristics, and quality of the final product. In the process they continually negotiate with the writer. Of course, authors are ultimately in charge of their product. But the editor is the coach and the expert at this point. With this degree of influence over the finished writing an argument might be made for the characterization of the editor as Principal.

4

Aaron and Moses

The Biblical story of Aaron and Moses has everything—acts of God, horrible events, miracles, betrayal, and punishment. There is also great love—of God for the people of Israel and of the brothers for each other. Moses may be the most notable figure in the Old Testament. He was chosen by God to lead his people out of Egyptian enslavement. God spoke directly to him. He was empowered by God to speak to the Jewish people. The only difficulty was that he did not speak well. He needed help. And God turned to Moses' brother to perform the role of spokesperson.

In addition to this role of spokesperson, the brother, Aaron, also performed other functions. He became the chief priest, performed miracles, and supported Moses as leader. All of these roles and the fact that it was God who sent Aaron to the aid of his brother might support a claim that Aaron is the ultimate Second Fiddle.

Another side of Aaron emerged in the progress of the two brothers in escaping from slavery in Egypt, through the Wilderness, to the point of getting ever so close to the Land of Milk and Honey. As well as supporting Moses he also betrayed him, and God, on occasion, and despite being called a great mediator, he was also considered by some students to be weak and, according to his worst critics, as being totally ineffective.

But before getting too deeply into how helpful Aaron was as the aide to his Principal, Moses, the story of the trials of the two brothers must be given. It is not an unpleasant task, although some parts are a bit unsettling, because these two men, coming together at ages eighty-three, Aaron, and eighty, Moses, experienced one of the greatest adventures ever recorded. In fact, few fictional journeys can match what happened to them in their forty years travelling together.

Moses and Aaron: earlier days

Pharaoh feared that the people of Israel who were slaves to the Egyptians were becoming so numerous as to be a threat, so he ordered the slaves' male children to be killed. Moses' mother floated the child in a basket to where Pharaoh's daughter found him. The daughter arranged for Moses' mother to raise him, and later the daughter took Moses as her son. He matured and did well until he killed an Egyptian who was mistreating a Hebrew slave. Moses, fearing for his life, fled to the land of the Midianites, the Sinai Wilderness, far away from Pharaoh, and began life as a shepherd. He prospered, married, and had children.

God came to Moses while he was tending his flock and called upon Moses to return to Egypt and secure the escape of the Jewish people. Moses gave excuses, but God was persistent and armed Moses with miracles to win over the Jewish leaders. God assured Moses that He would be behind him in his encounters with Pharaoh. Moses' final excuse was that he did not speak well, but God offered his brother, Aaron, as spokesperson. Moses returned with his family to Egypt.

Aaron had remained in Egypt, raised a family, and had become influential in the Jewish community. Hebrew tradition held that Aaron was a peacemaker who believed in conciliation as a way of settling disputes among his people. God told Aaron to go into the wilderness and meet Moses. When they met after their long separation, Moses told Aaron of the task that God had given them.

Dealing with Pharaoh

The two brothers went to Pharaoh with the "Let my people go" plea, saying that the people wished only to go into the wilderness to hold a feast for their God. Pharaoh refused. Moses and Aaron then requested that their people be allowed to go three days' journey into the wilderness in order to perform sacrifices to God. Pharaoh again refused, at the same time making their lives harder by refusing to give them straw for their brick-making duties. This he did by ordering them to gather their own straw, still requiring the same output.

The brothers, whom God gave the task of leading the Hebrew people out of Egypt, went again before Pharaoh. God had given them the ability to perform miracles. Moses told Aaron to throw down his rod before Pharaoh; Aaron did so and it became a serpent. Pharaoh's magicians replicated the miracle, but Aaron's serpent swallowed the serpents of the magicians. Still Pharaoh said no.

In order to convince Pharaoh to release their people, Aaron and Moses took advantage of God's offer of a variety of plagues, ten in all, to be imposed upon the Egyptians. Aaron caused the waters of the Nile to turn to blood. This did not move Pharaoh. Then either Aaron or Moses or both are credited with resorting to a variety of plagues. They began with frogs, gnats, and afflictions upon cattle. These acts were followed by a fine dust that caused boils. Then came hail, locusts, and three days of darkness. The plagues caused harm to the Egyptians but not the Israelites. Still, after each devastating event, Pharaoh would not relent.

In a final effort Moses told the Jewish slaves to put the blood of lambs upon their two doorposts and their lintels. This would be a sign that would cause God to spare their children as he dealt death upon the firstborn of the Egyptians. This final action provided the impetus for the Egyptians to relent and drive the Israelites from the land. The visitors had lived there four hundred years.

Forty years of wandering

While the Israelites were freed from the terrible slavery they had suffered for so long, they began a trek of wandering through the desert of Sinai that brought severe hardship upon the people and tested the leadership of Aaron and Moses. The first setback was the Egyptians' wanting their slaves to return and pressed Pharaoh to follow the escapees. The situation appeared dire as they came to the Red Sea, but God caused an east wind to rise and push back the sea. This provided a path of safety on the dry bottom for the former slaves. Then, when the sea rolled back the forces of Pharaoh were doomed.

Although the people were no longer pursued, they experienced extensive hardship in the next forty years of wandering back and forth in the harsh Sinai desert. They lacked food and water and made demands upon Aaron and Moses to help them. At the same time many wished they had never left Egypt. When these "murmurs" became intense, the Lord appeared in a cloud and provided a type of bread, called manna, and also sufficient quail to satisfy their hunger. Moses struck a rock and water emerged to assuage their thirst.

Fierce nomadic Amalek warriors attacked the wanderers and Moses sent Joshua to repel them. When Moses held up his hands on the battlefield Amalek were dispersed, but when he lowered his hands the tide of battle turned, so Aaron and another leader held up Moses' arms when he became tired.

Moses went up on Mount Sinai to receive the Ten Commandments. While he was gone, the people did not know what had become of him and demanded that Aaron make gods to see them through their arduous journey. In the lowest point of his support for Moses Aaron acceded to their wishes and made a figure of a calf out of gold that was brought to him. Upon his return Moses was furious. He smashed the tablets containing the laws and destroyed the calf. He criticized Aaron severely for bringing shame upon the people; however, he obtained God's forgiveness for Aaron and the people, and the trek continued.

Aaron: Chief Priest

While on Mount Sinai Moses received detailed instructions for constructing the sanctuary and the Ark of the Law. Major dual roles were designated for Aaron as the Chief Priest. He was to make intercession for the people to God and also to transmit God's will to the people. He and his male descendants were to be perpetual priests and were granted preferred positions in and around the sanctuary and the Ark when it was carried along as the people moved and when it was retired each night. Aaron and his sons were to conduct the religious ritual for the Israelites.

Aaron's vestments were to be designed according to an ordained plan, and his ordination as Chief Priest was to be performed according to an established ritual. He and his heirs were to receive certain perpetual dues from the people, such as moneys forfeited for violating God's rules and choice parts of the meat and other offerings by the people to their God.

Aaron had numerous other duties. He conducted a census of the Hebrew people, tribe by tribe. He presided over the various offerings, such as the burnt offering, the sin offering, and the peace offering. For instance, in the peace offering he was required to kill the ox and the ram and throw their blood upon the altar. At the same time there were rules for his maintaining the cleanliness of his vestments.

He passed on to the people the laws that God gave to Moses and administered the punishment for the violation of codes of conduct. Numerous rules applied to the personal conduct of the priests and of the people. Aaron was at the center of all of these rules, making him, according to students of the period, similar to a king in importance.

Murmurs and miracles

Throughout Aaron and Moses' adventures together numerous resentments and objections to their leadership arose from the Hebrew people. The privations endured in the Wilderness were very difficult, from climate, travel hardships, and lack of food and water. It was fortunate that Moses was capable of speaking directly to God without any intermediary. He could obtain God's help for the suffering of the people, as when God provided quail and manna from heaven when the people were starving.

The rebellions against Moses' leadership also came from individuals in the Hebrew camp. One of these murmurs came from an unexpected source: his brother, Aaron, and his sister, Miriam. Miriam was older than the brothers and according to tradition she was the person who observed Pharaoh's daughter's finding the baby Moses. Miriam also is said to have arranged for the baby to be raised for a period of time by her mother.

Aaron and Miriam, both prophets of the Lord, gave two complaints against Moses. The lesser complaint was that he had married a Cushite, or Ethiopian, woman. Their major concern was that Moses was the only person to speak for God and that they did not. God then met with the three siblings and told them that he spoke to prophets in visions and dreams, but that he spoke to Moses "mouth to mouth." God punished Miriam for her rebellion by giving her leprosy, but relented after a plea for mercy by Moses, and Miriam was soon cured.

After the rebellion Aaron staged with his sister, both remained faithful to Moses throughout their lives. The brothers' joint leadership efforts were resented by some of the Levites and others, especially because of the brothers' being the only ones to represent the people before God. The Lord vindicated Aaron and Moses by causing the earth to swallow up the rebels and by bringing a plague upon the Israelites. The plague was halted only upon Aaron's making atonement for the people before the Lord.

The Promised Land—almost

When the people neared their destination, the Lord told Moses to send representatives of all the tribes to investigate the nature of the land and its inhabitants, and whether those native persons would give much resistance. The spies returned and reported that they had indeed seen a land of Milk and Honey, but the people there were strong, and the country was well-fortified and difficult to invade. Upon hearing this Moses' people determined that they should select new leaders who would lead them back to Egypt.

The Lord was infuriated by this and threatened to destroy the Israelites. Moses interceded and the Lord pardoned the people; however, he vowed that none of the people over the age of twenty who had "murmured" against him would be permitted to enter the destination, Canaan. He did except Caleb and Joshua, who had been faithful, from this edict.

The Levites, who assisted the priests in their duties, staged a revolt against the leadership of Moses and Aaron. The Levites desired to be placed upon equal footing with the priests. The Lord was again furious and Moses pleaded on behalf of the rebels, but the Lord caused a plague to begin, in order to consume them. Moses ordered Aaron to make atonement on behalf of the complainers, but they still refused to obey the Lord. The Lord then told the people to stand back from the homes of the rebels. He made the earth open up and consume the rebels, along with their families and their homes.

The Lord wished to confirm the choice of Aaron and his sons as priests. The Lord told Moses to obtain a rod from each tribe and place it in the ground by the sanctuary overnight. In the morning Aaron's rod was adorned with blossoms and ripe almonds. The rod was placed in the tabernacle as a prevention against further rebellion.

Aaron's last days

A final revolt against Moses and Aaron occurred in the Wilderness over the lack of water for the congregation and their cattle. The Lord told the brothers to gather the people together. Moses was to tell a rock to send forth water for the people. Instead, Moses tapped the rock twice with a rod, and water came gushing out. The Lord told Moses and Aaron that because of this lack of faith and disobedience in not speaking to the rock, as ordered, they would not be permitted to enter Canaan.

Moses took Aaron and his son, Eleazar, to the top of Mount Hor, and, pursuant to the Lord's instructions, had Aaron's priestly robes placed upon Eleazar. This confirmed Eleazar as the Chief Priest.

Aaron died on the top of Mount Hor in his 123rd year, the fortieth of the remarkable adventure with his brother. He was mourned by the house of Israel for thirty days, the same length of time for which Moses was later mourned. Moses went on to lead the people to the Promised Land although he, like Aaron, was not permitted to enter.

The Importance of Aaron

There is no question that Aaron has outstanding strengths. Just the fact that he was chosen by God to support a central figure of the Old Testament—his brother Moses—establishes his credentials as an imposing figure.

He was the spokesman for Moses, God's leader of the Chosen People. He was to Moses as Moses was to God. Even though God spoke to Moses directly, "mouth-to-mouth," God spoke directly to Aaron on two occasions, in Leviticus 10:8 and Numbers 18:1 and following verses.

Aaron was designated by God as Chief Priest, beginning a priestly lineage that lasted, with interruptions, for a thousand years. As chief priest, he was an intermediary between the people and God. He took naturally to mediating and peacekeeping.

Aaron was well provided-for in his role as Chief Priest. He and the other priests received the tributes and penalties due from the people to God. Priests were to have a share of the meat and the other food dedicated to God in the various offerings required pursuant to religious ritual. Aaron's robes as Chief Priest were splendid in their colors and various insignia of office-fit for a king. This was appropriate since he held kingly secular and ecclesiastical power.

He was "there at the beginning," older than Moses, but more importantly, was with Moses from the start of Moses' recruitment by God, through trials and victories, to ever-so-close to reaching the Land of Milk and Honey.

He roused the Hebrew people to leave Egypt, and helped convince Pharaoh to let the people go, even to the extent of participating in bringing on the ten plagues. With his rod he performed the miracles of God, and had a hand in providing manna and drink in the Wilderness.

Aaron's weaknesses

The forty-year adventures of Aaron and his brother Moses provided numerous opportunities for failure. He was a human being with all the frailty that implied. Perhaps it is fortunate that his missteps were not more numerous.

In the beginning he was, at eighty-three, hesitant to engage in the lofty task God expected of him. As a mediator and man of peace such active roles as assisting in plagues and helping lead his people through hardships and rebellion were foreign to his nature.

The pressure of the Israelites' "murmurs" while Moses was up on the mountain receiving the Ten Commandments, was especially stressful for Aaron. Given his nature the course that he chose to meet the emergency was to go along with their demands for a god that they could see.

What emerged was a golden calf—an earthly "god" that proved to be his greatest error and caused the greatest criticism. Moses was furious about Aaron's failure to maintain God's plan while Moses was absent on the mountain.

The rebellion staged by Aaron along with his sister Miriam was another sign of his lack of support for his brother in their mission. As prophets he and Miriam staged a resistance, possibly grounded in jealousy toward their brother's favored role in relating directly to God.

For this rebellion, the golden calf episode, and other lapses, some critics have strongly condemned Aaron for his jealousy of Moses, his failure to support his brother, and his straying from God's plan for his people. It has been contended that he was not fit to wear the priestly robes.

What sort of Second Fiddle was Aaron?

Perhaps nowhere in history has one person given support for so long, through so many trying conditions, as Aaron provided Moses. Beginning at age eighty-three, for the next forty years Aaron traveled beside his brother. Unaware of the extensive time that the Hebrew people would wander in the wilderness, Aaron would not have known when he signed on that the task would take so terribly long.

However, he could assume from the first that the going would be very difficult. Escaping from the power house that was Egypt was a significant challenge. After this the Red Sea, the battles with enemy armies along the way and the privations of desert travel were more than any but the strong could provide support for another person. Certainly the rebellious sentiments of the people following Moses added to the unpleasantness of the task of being an effective Second Fiddle. In spite of the trials of this long-term commitment, Aaron stayed on with his Principal until death overtook him. Aaron did receive many honors. In addition to being a part of the leadership team of his people, he was made Chief Priest of his nation at a time when government and religion were one. And the honor was perpetual in that his sons succeeded to the priestly leadership.

Some critics in evaluating Moses' relationship with his brother have said that Moses may have been jealous of the fact that Aaron had sons to continue his line and Moses did not. The fact that Aaron's sons also may have been chosen to continue the priestly line may also have bothered Moses. Of course, Aaron along with his sister Miriam, also exhibited a jealous reaction to Moses' special relationship with God.

These slippages in the relations between siblings are not unheard of. Moses and Aaron's sharing of stressful, dangerous, and demanding tasks over such a long period of time might have been expected to lead to even more disagreements and abrasive behavior than the record indicates as having actually occurred.

Aaron, through this journey from slavery to nearly reaching the Promised Land, proved to be a Second Fiddle of the first caliber and worthy of emulating.

5

Lou Gehrig and Babe Ruth

In a sports page column "This Date in Baseball" appears the following note: "1930: Lou Gehrig drove in eight runs with a grand slam and two doubles as the New York Yankees outlasted the Boston Red Sox 14–13." Gehrig performed at this level of playing year after year with the Yankees from 1925 to 1939, amassing records, Most Valuable Player, All-Star, and other honors. And, during that period he played for a total of 2,130 consecutive games.

In light of this career of one of the greatest baseball players of all time, how can it be said that Lou Gehrig could play Second Fiddle to anyone? Perhaps the task of proving that he was Second Fiddle to Babe Ruth is impossible, or possible only in a very limited way of looking at the typical Second Fiddle.

First, the lives of both baseball greats will be set out in some detail. Consideration will be given to their early upbringing and education along with individuals who influenced their personalities and abilities. Their personalities could not have been more different and affected their playing and their relationships with others, especially women. Their careers on some of the great ball teams of all time will be described, with the inevitable highs and lows they experienced.

After both are introduced their relationship will be explored. In this relationship will lie evidence as to whether one of these strong individuals could have been dominant or subservient in any sense of those terms. Perhaps some alternate ways of looking at the roles of Principal and Second Fiddle will be necessary in this relationship of such heroic figures. Perhaps it will prove futile to enlist Lou Gehrig, the Iron Horse, as a Second Fiddle.

Lou Gehrig: Early Years

Lou was born in 1903 into a German immigrant family. His father was often without work but was influential in stressing the importance of conditioning. His mother was a maid and later a cook at a fraternity house at Columbia University. She was the consistent breadwinner in the family. She emphasized to Lou the importance of hard work.

Lou was very close to his family all of his life, living with them until nearly the time of his marriage. He was especially close to his mother, relying upon her for rules and stability well into his adulthood. She wished for him a career in architecture and engineering and was not supportive of his baseball playing.

Lou was not a natural at sports, even though he played many of them. He was strong enough, but he came by his skills through hard work and repetition. In high school he played soccer, football, and baseball. In baseball he had the additional handicap of being a lefthander.

He could hit the long ball. While on his high school baseball trip to Chicago, Lou hit a homer over the fence at the Cubs field. A newspaper of the day compared him at that early time with the already-established Babe Ruth. Even though Lou was a Giant fan he had begun a life-long habit of looking up to the Babe. Ruth influenced many players to swing for the fences.

He enrolled in Columbia University and was a pitcher on the baseball team. He had a fastball but his control was unpredictable. In the summer of 1921 he played professionally for the Hartford Senators under an assumed name. He was suspended from playing for Columbia for a year and resumed in 1923, gaining a 6 and 4 record in pitching and hitting .444.

Career in Baseball

Paul Krichell, a Yankee scout, believed he had found in Gehrig the next Babe Ruth and gave his opinion to manager Ed Barrow. Barrow made Lou an offer and Lou began his illustrious career. He experienced much success with the Hartford farm team, hitting 37 home runs and batting .369. He was brought up to the Yankee squad for the last game of 1924.

On June 2, 1925, manager Miller Huggins put Gehrig in at first base for Wally Pipp who had played that position for ten years. This began "The Streak" that would be followed by fans for years and earn Gehrig the name "Iron Horse." As the Iron Horse he was thought of as a steady, strong locomotive who propelled the Yankees to fame and success on the playing field.

Some commentators would say that the Streak was not of prime concern to Gehrig, but in reality he indicated on various occasions how he treasured it. He would correct those who gave the incorrect number of successive games he had played. He no doubt was fully aware of it when he kept himself in the lineup with aches and pains, broken bones, and the advancing stages of the disease of ALS, to which he finally succumbed.

After a successful 1926 season Lou contributed mightily to the 1927 Yankees, thought by some to be the greatest baseball team of all time. Not only did it feature Gehrig and the immensely popular and talented Babe Ruth, but the team's hitting strength earned it the name "Murderers' Row." The team's star power helped overcome the "Black Sox" scandal of seven years before, and set the course for the overwhelming popularity of baseball as a national sport.

Gehrig and Ruth added a huge dimension to the interest in baseball that year with a "Home Run Derby" that would be followed intently by baseball fans. The sport had developed from an emphasis upon hitting singles to an appreciation for the long ball. Of course, Ruth had provided the home runs that whetted by fans' appetite for more. During the 1927 season the fans got what they wanted. Ruth hit one, then Gehrig; Ruth hit two in a game, and Gehrig matched them the next day. Observers were not certain who might win the race in the end. It was not until the latter part of the season that Lou fell behind, perhaps because of his concern for an illness that had befallen his mother. He still had a very successful year with 47 home runs to Ruth's record-breaking 60. Gehrig earned the Most Valuable Player award with a record 174 runs batted in and a .373 average. Ruth had 164 RBI's and .356, but of course still "stole the show" with the huge homer total and his usual dominant personality and reputation.

Gehrig continued through his career to work at being in fine physical shape, being prepared to play, and going over the top in hustle. These attributes caused him to be a leader by example on the team and eventually to be named team captain. He was not a leader in the usual sense. He was found to be aloof by his teammates, but this did not indicate that he did not care for them or their well-being.

To the contrary, he showed his concern for various members through occasional gifts and even having them over to have his mother cook them a meal.

His strength was such that he could and indeed preferred to power the ball directly out over the head of the infielder without the aid of a friendly wind to assist. He practiced his position until he made few errors. His style was minimalist—efficient in both his work on the field and at bat.

In spite of this efficiency he did have his rituals. He smoothed the ground around first base with the toe of his spikes; he spat on his hands when batting; and then there was the habit with the chewing gum. At the beginning of each season he gave to a trainer numerous packs of gum. The trainer then doled out to him a stick of gum for each game. Of course, two sticks would be forthcoming for a double-header.

His aloofness in the locker-room and on the bench was a symptom of his natural shyness and lack of gregariousness. These attributes extended to his relationship with women. He was close to his mother, taking her to spring training, sending her gifts from road trips, and living at home. His mother's protectiveness extended to the prevention of Lou's becoming involved with women. His mother's reach ended, however, when he met Eleanor Grace Twitchell.

He met Eleanor, from the South Side of Chicago, on the night before the third game of the 1932 World Series. Uncharacteristically of him, the eternal wallflower at parties, he offered to get Eleanor a drink, talked with her, and walked her home. They were married by the mayor of New Rochelle, New York, on September 29, 1933. He was faithful to Eleanor until his death, while at the same time continuing to revere his mother. The relationship of Eleanor and his mother was fraught with acrimony, even in the days of his last illness.

He continued to be the premier baseball player of the 1930's, especially as Babe Ruth grew older and heavier and slowed down, eventually being traded to the Boston Braves in 1935. Gehrig continued with his exemplary play at first base, extraordinary extra-base hitting, and leadership of the Yankees. He was honored with accolades for all of these things, and, considering his great strength and conditioning, appeared to be destined for a long-term career.

ALS

His baseball career was cut short with the onset of amyotrophic lateral sclerosis in 1938. At first it showed in blisters and bruises on his hands, then trouble with balance, and finally the sapping of strength. This led to the decline of his skills on the field and at the plate, except for occasional reoccurrences of his old self. The latter were often the result of sheer will power on his part.

Disbelief among the fans, and then derision, were followed, when his condition was understood, by silence and support. He continued to show up for games, play even when his manager, Joe McCarthy, told him to rest, and added to The Streak. He hit his last home run against Dutch Leonard in Washington on September 27, 1938. It was number 493. His last RBI was on April 25, 1939—number 1995.

Later in the spring he told his manager that he would sit out a couple of games. The manager, Joe McCarthy, told Babe Dahlgren to start in place of Gehrig at first base. Dahlgren could not believe that Lou Gehrig was no longer the first baseman of the New York Yankees. Nor could anyone in baseball. Gehrig had held that position for 2130 games in a row, much of the time without even a back-up first baseman. Manager Joe McCarthy had Gehrig take the lineup to the home plate umpire so that he could receive the applause of the crowd.

Gehrig was diagnosed with ALS at the Mayo clinic, and was told to stop playing baseball. He did not want sympathy, so that for a time only those closest to him knew the seriousness of his illness.

On July 4, 1939, the Yankees scheduled the Lou Gehrig Appreciation Day during a doubleheader with the visiting Washington Senators. In addition to the overflow crowd at Yankee Stadium, the 1927 team held a reunion.

Gehrig had to be coaxed to speak by Joe McCarthy. When Gehrig finally agreed, he gave perhaps the best-known speech in the history of sport. He told of how he felt that "Today I consider myself the luckiest man on the face of the earth." He said that the fans had never offered him anything but support. He further listed those persons, teammates, opponents, family, and his wife who had shown him nothing but "kindness and encouragement." He went on to list those with whom he had been privileged to spend his career. These persons included league officials, teammates, opponents, family, and his wife.

In retirement he became a commissioner on the New York City Parole Board. He attended Yankee games and sat on the bench. His number 4 was retired in late 1939 and he was elected to the Hall of Fame that same year.

He went through the latter stages of ALS showing his usual strength and, at first, optimism. His major symptom was loss of power in his muscles. In the end he succumbed on June 2, 1941. At his viewing an endless line of mourners, including Ruth, passed his casket.

Babe Ruth: Early Years

The Babe was born in Baltimore, Maryland, and lived in his early life in the dock area of Baltimore Harbor. His father was a salesman and owned a succession of taverns. His mother had eight children, six of whom died early. She lived only until age thirty-two. Ruth's life was one of lack of permanency or supervision.

His father turned George Herman over to the care of the Zaverian order at the St. Mary's Industrial School for Boys where he stayed until age twenty. That school was the home of eight hundred boys many of which were assigned there as delinquents. The training was mainly vocational, such as carpentry, baking, and gardening. There was very little classroom teaching.

The school was known for its baseball. The boys played all the time, under the supervision of Brother Matthias, a giant of a man, whom Ruth looked up to for the rest of the Brother's life. Brother Matthias regularly batted fly balls to the boys. It has been suggested that the upward swing necessary to cause the arc of the ball had a strong influence on the Babe's motion at swinging the bat toward the fences. His hitting style contrasted with that of Lou Gehrig who was more of a line drive home run hitter.

Ruth's personality was loud and boisterous, with little restraint on his actions. This reflected his earlier unsupervised years. Even at St. Mary's he never seemed to understand the usual boundaries on what he could do. Except for periods of time when he became so low in strength and spirit and when he was under the control of his second wife, he would be the life of the party, the leader and participant in outrageous behavior. This, of course, was in sharp contrast with his conservative, predictable teammate, Lou Gehrig.

A star at the age of eighteen, he was picked up by the Baltimore Orioles in 1913 at a salary of $250 a month. On the train to spring training in Fayetteville, North Carolina, he was talked into placing his arm in the net for valuables in the sleeping berth. This practical joke, however, paled in comparison with his lifetime of playing tricks on others, including nailing a player's shoes to the floor.

He was soon sold to the Boston Red Sox where he attained fame as an outstanding fastball pitcher. In 1916, for instance, he had a league-leading 1.75 earned run average and a record nine shutouts. In 1917 he completed 35 games in 41 starts. In the World Series of 1916 and 1918 he pitched 25 2/3 scoreless innings.

In spite of his success as a pitcher he wanted to be an outfielder or first baseman, but Manager Ed Barrow opposed the change. He quit the team in protest in 1918 but returned to play center field. As a player he began his career-long string of hitting the longest ball hit in numerous ball parks in and out of the United States. These prodigious hits and lots of them were a significant change to baseball. The game before the Ruth era had been like chess matches, filled with strategic decisions. The ball was soft and the bats were insufficient for the long ball. This change with Ruth as, year after year, he hit more homers. He was known as the Colossus, Mauler, and Home Run King.

In Boston he met and married a pretty waitress, Helen Woodford. Even with this change of responsibility which kept him out of military service in World War I, on the road his lifestyle of indulgence and excess in food, drink, swearing, and even women, continued.

The 1920 sale of Ruth by the Red Sox owner caused an uproar of criticism by the Boston fans. While Ruth's behavior was given as reason for the trade, possibly the main reason was the need for money to fund the play *No, No, Nannette*. The price of the sale was $125,000, paid by Colonels Rupert and Huston, Yankee owners.

The Babe and the Yankees

From 1920 to 1935 Babe Ruth played for the New York Yankees, hitting some of the high points in baseball, and, as usual with the Babe, experiencing some setbacks and lows. The 1920's, Ruth, New York City, and the Yankees were made for each other. Until the 1929 crash the era of prosperity and optimism, of winning and not looking back, of success of the Bronx Bombers, was to be found in New York City as nowhere else.

Babe Ruth was the greatest name in baseball. He sold the tickets. He filled the sports pages and sometimes the news pages, too. He hit the home runs. He still did the outrageous things, but the public seemed forever ready to forgive and even like his "bad boy" image.

When he was good, he was very, very good. He continued his home run production, reaching a high of sixty in 1927 and stopping finally in 1935 with a total of 714. He also maintained a strong batting average and supported the team with respectable RBI's.

His star quality, while annoying to some of his teammates yielded him privileges given to no others. He had his own phone in the locker room and his own drawing room on the travel train. He earned the highest salaries. He wined and dined with the elite. He was mobbed in New York and on the road and overseas during barnstorming tours at the end of the seasons.

His continuously being in motion, day and night, his outrageous appetites, and his philandering predictably led to lows—illness, moodiness, and lowered production on the ball field. When he finally hit the bottom of poor health and spirit, he had various means of climbing back up again. He spent one summer getting in shape on the farm he and his wife Helen owned. Another rejuvenation was performed in a well-known gym in New York.

It was his second wife, Claire, who brought the greatest amount of order to his life, and even then, when they were apart he would fall back on old bad habits. He and his first wife, Helen had divorced and Helen perished in a fire in early 1929. Even while married Ruth began living with Claire and married her in April, 1929. Claire monitored the Babe's dress and manners, and as time went on exercised control over the various financial dealings in which he was involved.

Numerous honors came to the Babe. He was the first American League Most Valuable Player and would have repeated except in the early days one could earn the award only once. He was admitted to the first class of the Baseball Hall of Fame, along with Ty Cobb, Honus Wagner, and Christy Mathewson. He was feted at Babe Ruth Day at Yankee Stadium in April, 1947. His number 3 was retired in June, 1948. These formal recognition events were, of course, in addition to the cheering for his heroic feats of hitting and the numerous records that he achieved over his twenty-two year career.

Legends emerged naturally around this legendary figure. While it was disputed whether he really liked kids or not, more than once he was credited with saving the life of a child or improving their health through promising them a homer and delivering on his promise.

Lou Gehrig had been in awe of the Babe long before Gehrig joined the Yankees in 1925. He had been called the "High School Babe Ruth" and the "Next Babe Ruth." Lou continued to be deferential to the Babe, as, when someone wanted a picture of them together, Lou would say it was okay with him if it was okay with the Babe. He endured kidding by the Babe about his very ordinary life style, while the Babe wished to party. Lou would, however, get irritated when they partnered at bridge on the long train rides during the season. The Babe delighted in making outrageous bids to get under Gehrig's skin.

Even their places in the lineup during their most productive years together had the appearance of deference on Lou's part. Miller Huggins, the manager, made some changes in the spring of 1927. While in 1926 Ruth was third, Bob Meusel fourth, and Gehrig fifth, the order for '27 was Gehrig following Ruth and Meusel fifth. In the words of Leigh Montville in *The Big Bam*: "Gehrig had moved into position to protect Ruth, a backup force to be feared. Walk Ruth? A pitcher knew then he would have to face Gehrig with a man on first." (Page 256)

The productive, close association between these two baseball heroes suffered a five-year hiatus beginning about 1934. Various causes have been given for the animosity between the two. One was a comment that Lou's mother made to the Babe's wife, Claire, regarding her supposed favoritism of her natural daughter, Julia, over her adopted daughter, Dorothy. This episode was said to have reached the two men. Another view was that Lou had found his wife, Eleanor, in Ruth's stateroom on the ship during the trip to Japan in the 1934 barnstorming tour. Whatever the reason, they did not speak until the Lou Gehrig Appreciation Day in 1939.

Whether or not the years of excesses were the cause, the years began to catch up with the Babe in the early thirties. He gained weight, began drinking more heavily, and became less reliable in the field, while, however, still hitting home runs. As his abilities waned the Yankee ownership were less supportive of him and his demands.

Ruth had for years wished to manage the Yankees, and had been repeatedly turned down. The final break came when he indicated his desire to manage in 1935, even though Joe McCarthy was already on the job. The Yankee management said no again and Ruth left in a huff. He decided to quit the team with which he was so identified.

The Braves and the End
The Boston Braves, sensing his continuing star value, offered him a contract that included playing, some management responsibilities, and other enticements. He found the promises to be hollow and so played only a limited number of games for the Braves in the early 1935 season. His last day came in Pittsburgh when he went out heroically, hitting three home runs for a last hurrah. He quit the Braves team in June, 1935.

He kept himself busy in his retirement in occasional ball games, usually with amateurs, and being the attraction at celebrations and competitions. He accepted the honors of having his number retired, Cooperstown Hall of Fame induction, and Babe Ruth Day at Yankee Stadium.

He showed up for the Lou Gehrig Day at the Stadium as a member of the great 1927 team. The two greats were together, and the Babe stepped forward to give Gehrig a hug that apparently went a long way to healing their five-year feud. After Gehrig's passing Ruth appeared at his viewing and was moved to tears at the coffin.

The Babe became ill in late 1946; he had cancer. With radiation he managed to get somewhat better and was able to attend Babe Ruth Day, the 1947 World Series, and the retiring of his number 3 in a reunion of the 1923 team. Babe Ruth died on August 16, 1948, at the age of 53.

Was Gehrig a Second Fiddle to Babe Ruth?

In answer to this question we must first look to the definition of a Second Fiddle: One who is capable, loyal, and energetic, and who is willing to take on perhaps a big part of the task—and who is willing not to be the leader. We will consider the pros and cons of this issue and then arrive at a conclusion.

On the positive side Gehrig is very often thought of, although extremely talented, as second to Ruth as a ballplayer and as a part of the great Yankee teams. A major reason for this is the public's infatuation with one statistic—the number of home runs. However, Gehrig did very well in chasing Ruth's homer output, even taking the country by storm in the 1927 "Derby." In Gehrig's mind, his "Baby" was the run batted in, in which he typically exceeded Ruth. Another consideration is that the Bambino was the hero of the 1920's and Gehrig was the Iron Horse of the 1930's as well as the late '20's. The result of this is that it is from the perspective of largely later generations who have seen Gehrig as Second Fiddle. Even here, perhaps the better term would be that Gehrig was considered "Second Banana" to Ruth's starring role.

Gehrig's loyalty to Ruth was constant until the time of their "split" that lasted for five years until Gehrig's illness. Lou's loyalty to Ruth continued through times when the Babe was, in a reflection of his personality, dismissive, rude, and inconstant. The loyalty trait in Lou was part of his way of life and his personality and was reflected in his consideration for his family, especially his mother, his managers, and the Yankees. In the case of Ruth, Lou's deference had its roots in his earliest baseball performance when he saw Ruth already established as a hero of the game and from the time that Gehrig began to be compared with Ruth.

Gehrig certainly was willing to be supportive of Ruth in the task of winning ball games. He did this in a concrete way as a result of Miller Huggins' changing the lineup so that Lou followed the Babe. This required opposing pitchers to pitch to Ruth because if they walked him they would find themselves being hit by Gehrig with a man (Ruth) on base. The result was a greater output by the Babe for a major portion of the two players' time together on Yankee teams.

But another way of looking at the SF question is that Gehrig's game-playing efforts were mainly directed toward the good of the team and its winning, and only incidentally in making the Babe more productive.

Certainly Lou Gehrig did not desire to be a leader. He was shy in his relationships with women, his teammates, and the public. This trait was especially noticeable when contrasted with the Babe's boisterousness. He was made captain of the Yankees after Ruth had left the team, but did not take naturally to that position at first. So he certainly had the Second Fiddle's characteristic of being a follower for most of his career. But it must be noted that his unwillingness to be the leader was not related especially to the Babe, as would be the case in the ordinary Second Fiddle-Leader situation.

In balance, during the time when Ruth and Gehrig were significant figures in Major League Baseball, the case can be made that Gehrig possessed some of the characteristics of the Second Fiddle. This conclusion is made regarding only the relationship between these two men and does not in any way reduce his comparative stature as the splendid Iron Horse of the New York Yankees.

6

Robert and John F. Kennedy

Few real-life stories have caught and held the public attention to the extent of Robert F. Kennedy and his brother, John F. Kennedy. There was youth that succeeded the Eisenhower World War II maturity, a long-held dream of attainment of the presidency, loyalty to family, and fierce brotherly protection and advancement. But nothing about the era of the New Frontier and the relationships of the Kennedys was simple. And with the continuous confusion of complexities came myths that were fostered then and are still strongly held today.

This complex, myth-filled body of lore has settled especially on the relationship Robert had with his older brother, John. The reputation of devotion to family is, of course, true; but was it total and unwavering? We know of the wide range of services rendered by Bobby to John, but how far did this rendition go, was it given ungrudgingly, and was it returned or compensated for? And we have heard by the loyal ties of this pair of brothers; can we say it was always honored as part of a two-way street? Behind these forces and questions lurked another unsettling consideration: the myth-making of father Joe and others that overlay the apparent Second Fiddle, Bobby, and his Principal, John.

Family

Joe Kennedy, Sr., had long wanted a son to be president, and the chosen son was the eldest, Joe, Jr. At least part of the motivation of this desire for family in high office was based upon earlier rejection of Joe, Sr., partly because of country of origin, Ireland, and sometimes because of religion, Roman Catholicism. Another factor was the aim of quieting the criticism of Joe, Sr.'s earlier reputed involvement in activities such as boot-legging.

Add a prior generation to the office-seeking. Both the Kennedy and the Fitzgerald grandfathers had played leadership roles in Boston politics. Perhaps this is unusual to have such political force affecting one family, but in areas of high immigrant population, the road to greater prosperity was often political. The early urban political organization has been called one of the earliest social service organizations, providing vital services to those who have little hope of otherwise gaining the American dream.

Father Joe's plan for the presidency did not die with the loss of the life of Joe, Jr. on a flying mission in World War II. The focus simply shifted to the next available son, John. And, to show how this order of responsibility worked, it has been suggested that Joe Sr. also urged Bobby to take appointments and other opportunities that would enhance his chances of high office.

In order to attain the highest office in the land one had to start on a lower rung of the political ladder. This rung was the United States House of Representatives, for which John ran in 1946. The next level up was the Senate in 1952, and finally the presidency in 1960. At every stage the corollary to the rule that each office must be won was that someone in the family had to take responsibility for the campaign. Only a family member could be trusted to make the commitment to the goal to be attained. This family member was Bobby. This desire by Joe Sr. that family be close by extended to appointments between elections, such as Jack's joining the Senate investigating committee on which Bobby was counsel, and Bobby's joining Jack's cabinet as Attorney General.

Bobby and Jack did all these things at the bidding of their father, but at least in the case of Bobby's being drafted into his brother's service, the presence of the father played a further role. Simply put, John and his father did not always get along, and when Joe leaned on him, he felt the need of someone to mediate—and the available buffer was Bobby. As Bobby gained success in organizing John's wins, he also gained Joe's respect for his organizational ability and Joe's gradually adopting a less prominent role in the campaigns. This trend, in turn, made Jack's life on the political trail and in office less stressful.

Bobby's role in the Kennedy "Family" extended beyond the heritage and political aims of his forebears and his brother. Throughout his tragically-shortened life he was the person his relatives relied upon in difficult times. In addition to all the other services he rendered to Jack, Bobby was there for Jackie at the time of loss of her child and loss of her husband. For this quality of taking charge for the benefit of his kin, she and other family members held Bobby in high regard.

Bobby

This younger brother's loyalty to the older is the basis of one of the most recognizable Second Fiddles to their Principals. He proved this loyalty in many public and private ways. But first, what was he "like," particularly in relation to his brother, and what effects did the responsibilities for service placed upon him have on his own personal goals and wishes? After all, selflessness, even embodied in such a reputation, cannot be completely one-sided, as research into the careers of Bobby and Jack has shown.

The Kennedy brothers' political association did not start out well. Jack was running for the House of Representatives in 1946 and Bobby was still in the Navy. Joe lobbied for Bobby's assisting in the campaign, but Jack was less than enthusiastic. In fact, he did not appear to want his brother around, reportedly asking an aide to take Bobby to Vaudeville or the movies.

RFK would not be deterred and assumed responsibility for working class areas of much lower stature and economic standing than the Kennedys. He had a knack for blending in with the persons in the assigned neighborhoods, however, playing ball and relating to them. The result was a much better showing for his brother in places where expectations had not been great.

JFK's reluctance to rely on his younger brother is not surprising. Both he and older brother Joe had been off to war when Bobby was growing up, so that Jack had a slanted perception of Bobby's abilities. Jack may also just not have wanted Bobby to be around, possibly resenting their father's "volunteering" the younger brother for the campaign.

Bobby had been raised in the shadows of two older brothers, both of whom became war heroes. He was smaller, even called "Runt," and had to strive in order to gain their respect. The well-known family penchant for competition made any hope of his attaining parity with his siblings even more difficult. Competition worked both ways, however. Although small, Bobby persevered to gain a football letter at Harvard, something his brothers had not attained.

While RFK was known in the years before his tragic end as being greatly concerned about the plight of the less fortunate and those lacking in the basic rights of citizens, his earlier regard for these persons and these matters reflected the conditions of his upbringing. By the time he was born, his father had attained significant wealth and the family lived very well. His father had attained social and political prominence, eventually being appointed Ambassador to the United Kingdom. Robert's education was pursued with young people of the wealthiest and most influential families. In addition to their educational reputations, his schools such as Milton Academy would support his efforts in gaining admission to Harvard University. He capped his educational career by studying law at the University of Virginia. From his upbringing and early experiences it is reasonable that he would not very much "feel the pain" of others lower down on the socioeconomic scale.

Similarities and differences

In spite of this lack of an appreciable amount of empathy it is rather ironic that Bobby took a positive position on the matter of civil rights before Jack. The irony is that the Kennedy Administration is publicly credited with an extreme sensitivity to guaranteeing to all the right to vote and perform other civic duties. Early in that Administration when the protest movement was forming, the brothers decided not to push for a civil rights bill or work very hard for the movement, at least in part because of their conclusion that such a bill would not pass, given the large southern influence in Congress at the time. Further, an emphasis upon civil rights would hamper the Administration's efforts on other legislation, as well as its chances of reelection.

Even more complex than the positions of the brothers on those less well off than themselves was the question of their relative "toughness" in dealing with others. Bobby's reputation is that of hard-charging and taking no prisoners in his efforts on behalf of his brother and in his own dealings. This, of course, permitted Jack to remain above the fray and not be sullied by the fall-out of campaign and other political handiwork.

Some of the close associates of the brothers have contradicted the public perceptions of the two. Close observers have said, for instance, that Bobby was very sensitive to the needs of staff and hesitant about firing individuals. Jack, on the other hand, could be ruthless in manner on occasion. An often quoted conclusion from Arthur Schlesinger, Jr., that sums up these contradictions is that the older brother was "a realist brilliantly disguised as a romantic," while the younger was "a romantic stubbornly disguised as a realist."

Related to the reputation for relentlessness that has attached to RFK is the perception that the Kennedy campaigns came off in the nature of "well-oiled machines." While associates say that Robert was unsparing of himself and others in the pursuit of his brother's election and of Jack's and his own agendas, these same observers and Bobby himself give another view. They say that much time and effort in the campaigns were spent in trial and error and in rectifying situations that had gone wrong.

Leadership experts would no doubt agree that moving the campaign or other political activity forward is better than giving the appearance of hesitation and second-guessing strategy and actions. This penchant for aggressively moving forward doubtless has fed the aura that has grown around Kennedy political activity. A further contributing factor was the myths that formed around the brothers and their actions.

Some of these myths of effectiveness and invincibility were consciously fostered by those associated with the brothers, with their father's active participation. Joe was particularly conscious of the importance of image. This characteristic was also found in Jack and was very helpful in his public career. And, given the attractiveness of the young, vital protagonists and their vigorous cohorts, the public and the press naturally furthered the illusions as they emerged.

A word about Bobby's bravado. This could be observed as he questioned witnesses when he was a congressional investigations committee counsel and as he dealt with those who would block Jack's political path. In the former case he not only demanded that important witnesses testify, but once they were before the rackets committees, he was aggressive in exposing their roles in questionable activities. Given RFK's past as the smallest in the family and ever trying to keep up, it took bravery to stand up to older, more experienced political and legal operatives. This profile of courage seemed to hold on most occasions, although one associate reported a television appearance in which Bobby was very much shaken and lacking in confidence. Even if this lack of confidence occurred very seldom, it underscores to an even greater extent the toll taken by his efforts on Jack's and his own behalf.

Services and loyalty

Loyal service is the prime characteristic of Bobby's role as Second Fiddle to his brother. Even though Bobby's contributions began at the behest of father Joe, they swelled beyond anything that even the family would have imagined. Even the role of "telling the truth"—not being a "yes man"—as a political and presidential advisor, if performed faithfully, is an ultimate rendition of service.

The matters of loyalty and service are so entwined that they are difficult to separate. Perhaps the best way to highlight these occasions of Bobby's assistance to his brother, sometimes at the cost of putting his own aims aside, is to include his actions in the events that entwined himself and Jack, which also often involved Joe, Sr., the family, and their associates.

Major milestones in the working life of the two brothers were Jack's various election campaigns. Also illuminating is their work together while Jack was in Congress and president, especially in investigations, civil rights, and the Cuba crises.

Campaigns

Jack's first run for office was for a House of Representatives seat from Massachusetts in 1946. Joe, Sr. was extremely active in this early campaign and proposed the involvement of his third son, Bobby. Jack was unimpressed and at first could see Bobby as valuable only in posing in his Navy uniform. After leaving the service Bobby volunteered to help and was given the wards of East Cambridge where Jack was least known and supported.

Bobby worked tirelessly and had an affinity for the working-class ethnic community. He clearly stated his preference of working alone without someone to guide him. As a result of his contributions to the winning campaign he gained the respect of both his father and brother.

When Jack ran against Henry Cabot Lodge, Jr., for a Senate seat in 1952, Joe was very much involved in every aspect of the campaign. He fired one of Jack's campaign aides and replaced him with Bobby who soon became manager. Bobby had been working in the Justice Department and as a prosecutor. With Bobby's entry Joe could move into the background, thus reducing the likelihood that his reputation for alleged past connections with criminals, for Wall Street dealings, and for bootlegging would harm the campaign. Joe performed the important role of moneybags and grew to trust Bobby's judgment.

Bobby created an alternative political organization side by side of the Massachusetts Democrats, and developed the reputation of being very good at running a campaign, especially since the 1952 campaign resulted in victory. The praise for his organizational ability is not unanimous, however. Others say that he was impatient, his ideas weren't always the best, and he lacked follow-through. An essential quality for winning in election after election, the will to win, was evident in 1952 and seemed to counter any perceived lack of organizational ability.

By his performance Bobby gained his brother's confidence to a degree not experienced before. Jack was also grateful to Bobby for guiding him to an electoral victory, as well as keeping their father at bay.

When Jack sought the position of vice president on Adlai Stevenson's 1956 Democratic ticket, Bobby had to put aside his work and ambition as counsel on an investigating committee in the Senate. This interruption was part of a pattern that started in 1952 and continued through Jack's final campaign. The tradition of the family called for all hands to help the political fortune of the eldest brother. In his efforts to elect Jack, Bobby, as next in line, was not neglected. Some of the positions Bobby received were likely designed to further his later availability and suitability for high political office.

Even though Jack lost the vice presidential appointment to Senator Estes Kefauver of Kentucky, Bobby gained presidential campaign organizational skills, including gathering delegates at the convention.

Bobby became chief counsel to a Senate investigations subcommittee. He had previously served as counsel to a Senate investigations committee under the leadership of Senators Joe McCarthy and John McClellan. With the subcommittee role he went after racketeering in the labor unions, beginning with the Teamsters. It was the hard-hitting investigation role that prompted Doris Kearns Goodwin to suggest that Bobby was acting out an "Oedipal urge" with respect to his father. This played out in his digging into issues that might cause his father's reputed past ties to organized crime to emerge in the course of the fact-finding. On the other hand, these ties of Joe's have been very difficult to prove, and it has been questioned whether Bobby had sufficient knowledge of possibly illegal relationships of his father.

Two issues involving his future emerged from his investigating tenure. In connection with concerns regarding his aggressive behavior in going after so-called "bad guys," brother Jack obtained appointment on the committee, leading some to say that Jack was there to keep his brother from going too far, thus ruining Jack's chances for the 1960 nomination. The significance for Second Fiddle-Principal relationships is that the Principal—Jack—took a role that would monitor the Second Fiddle—Bobby.

A second outcome of Bobby's work in investigations and that he gave as a reason for not taking the post of Attorney General in 1961 was that he was tired of going after the "bad guys."

Bobby was not anxious to become Jack's campaign manager for the 1960 presidential nomination and election. His personality was not conducive to the socializing and seeking of political favors, and he likely resented again placing his life and career on hold. He would be gaining more prominence, particularly in the event of another political victory for Jack, but the interruptions were not to his liking. Moreover, the two brothers had not grown close during the Rackets Committee hearings and the work on legislation designed to control the unions.

Bobby did accept the manager position in December, 1959, and ran the usual hard-charging campaign through the various state primaries. The high point was likely the storied victory in West Virginia with the frontal attack on the issue of the Catholicism of the candidate. This issue would also be raised rather than subdued during the election campaign. His experience in delegate gathering in 1956 paid off in the 1960 Democratic convention. Not concerned with his personal popularity but rather on getting the job done, Bobby was able to announce on the day of balloting that the campaign was within ten delegate votes of the number necessary for nomination.

In spite of RFK's claims to the contrary the perception of the election campaign in the fall of 1960 was that of the now-proverbial "well-oiled" variety. A significant feature was a very ambitious drive to register minorities. Joe worked behind the scenes, providing funding and strengthening Jack's resolve during the long ordeal.

The campaign brought the brother's closer together. Jack was very appreciative of his brother's selfless efforts. They had not previously socialized, partly because of differences in personality and to some extent because their wives did not get along exceptionally well. Jack and Bobby even entertained differently. Jack was said to be warmer at gatherings than his brother; Bobby had more difficulty or inclination to be the perfect host. However, Hickory Hill, home of Bobby and Ethel in Virginia, was the scene of assemblies of politicians and thinkers, as well as informal parties complete with tossing participants in the pool.

The President and the Attorney General

Bobby assisted in the serious work of preparing for the new administration, including the choosing of a cabinet. Joe very much wanted Bobby as Attorney General, thereby giving Bobby the same chance at high public office as had been given to Jack. Jack wanted him for his character and his organizational ability. It was thought that it would be better that Bobby be on the inside than being perceived as slipping in the side door when needed for consultation or help.

Bobby did not want the job, and turned it down. He did not want to do anything to spoil his brother's chances for success, and considered his concern for the plight of the Black minority to be a potential hazard to his brother. The Attorney General appointment was offered to Abraham Ribicoff and Adlai Stevenson, but they turned it down. Jack told Bobby that he should step up and make a "contribution" to the administration the same as others who were putting successful careers on hold to serve their nation. When Bobby finally accepted the nomination, significant opposition arose because of his being the brother of the President, his youth and lack of relevant legal experience, and his abrasive conduct in his past activities.

The nomination was approved, and Bobby became more in the cabinet than just the AG. He was the ever-present personal advisor. His occasional practice of remaining with the President at the end of meetings called to consider various topics, causing some to consider his power greater than appropriate. He was given long-term and special assignments when difficult matters arose, even in the area of foreign affairs. He and Ethel were assigned to go on a world-wide good-will tour designed to show a youthful dimension of the United States to persons overseas.

Cuba

After the failure of the 1961 Cuban invasion by exiles trained by the Central Intelligence Agency, Bobby assumed significant new roles in the area of foreign policy. He would be Jack's chief advisor on the island dictatorship, as Bobby was the person Jack had utter trust in. Bobby also took on the task of supervision of the CIA, and actively pursued the covert "Operation Mongoose" designed to overthrow the Castro regime. This operation would have utilized Cuban-run activities such as spying and sabotage. Bobby was anxious, as part of his perceived responsibility of protecting his brother, to bring about the fall of Castro and thus counter the criticism of the administration for the failure of the Bay of Pigs invasion.

Bobby was not a member of the National Security Council which advised the President on foreign affairs matters; however, he attended meetings of the group. When Soviet missiles were placed on the island of Cuba, the United States under President Kennedy demanded and secured their removal. During this time of severe tension an executive committee of the National Security Council was formed, consisting of defense and foreign affairs advisors. Although the committee had no formal head, Bobby became the de facto leader.

In this crisis, observers saw Bobby's uncanny ability to perceive Jack's point of view and to act on the President's behalf, enhancing the significant authority that the Attorney General already possessed. British historian Isaiah Berlin commented upon the "telepathic" contact between the two brothers.

Speaking on behalf of the principal office holder is a means for aides and staff members to gain power, not only in government but also in business, non-profits, and other realms of human activity. Since the subject matter of the activity or event is often so complex that the principal must parcel out oversight and negotiations, assistants are often in a position to assume roles and power that their "pay grade" simply does not warrant.

In his broad protective role during his foreign policy tenure Bobby used his force of personality as well as alter ego of the President to mitigate dissent among the foreign policy advisors. He was vigilant toward the events that could in some way harm Jack., and aggressively thwarted actions by those who might embarrass the President. As alter ego some observers thought Bobby acted as if he occupied the oval office as well as considered him to be the real occupant. General Maxwell Taylor declared that the extensive protection as it occurred between the Kennedys was a reversal of the usual situation where the older brother looks after the younger.

In the case of the President and the Attorney General, the handing off of responsibility apparently was genuine and in good faith. It was a result of a unique relationship between the two and was enhanced by the national emergencies that the brothers found themselves involved in.

Civil Rights

The relationship of the Second Fiddle to the Principal has perhaps never been so complex as in the case of RFK to JFK in the issue of civil rights for minority individuals. There was the relationship of brothers, of the President and the Attorney General, support and opposition in Congress and among the public, demonstrations and dramatic events in the South that inflamed the races, behind-the-scenes maneuvering and hesitating, as well as the usual myth-making of the Kennedy era.

Robert came earlier than his brother to the support of civil liberties for all Americans. He perhaps came in closer contact with average citizens in the course of his campaigning "on the ground." He likely understood the plight of the less powerful before Jack. JFK noted while he was President that he had not fully understood the concerns of minorities, and came to fuller realization of the problem through reading and study.

Bobby used a variety of tools to move the issue forward. He made speeches on civil rights, such as at the graduation of the first African-American students to attend the University of Georgia. He testified at critical times before Congress. He utilized the office of the Attorney General to enforce the Constitution and the laws and executive orders on social justice that had passed. Further, the actions of high officials of the Justice Department in negotiating enrollment of Black people in college and similar rights matters certainly could not have been done without the AG's support.

John F. Kennedy had made speeches on civil rights as a member of Congress in the 1950's. These speeches, however, went nowhere, given the political climate of the day. Significant opposition to enhancing economic, political, and social rights of Black people was prevalent in both North and South. Many of the strongest and most effective opponents were lodged in the senior committee members of the United States Senate and the House of Representatives.

During the early days of his administration President Kennedy made some strides in issuing executive orders that dealt with such topics as equality in employment and voting. African-Americans were appointed in larger numbers than ever before to positions in the government, including positions that did not deal with race or civil rights.

Bobby and others could not budge Jack to take the most crucial step in accomplishing equality for all Americans, that of proposing and supporting civil rights legislation for congressional passage. As President, Jack considered such a step to be detrimental to the success of other important bills, especially in light of the opposition of powerful congressional leaders of both South and North. He was also preoccupied with foreign affairs, a major, distinctive responsibility of the President.

Events moved both brothers to higher planes of support and action in the area of individual rights. Freedom

Rides in the South had their effect, as did moves to enroll Black people as students in such deep South universities as in Mississippi and Alabama. Marches for equal justice in such places as Birmingham advanced the movement.

Reactions to these advances came in the form of severe actions such as the killing of rights workers and even children, in the form of aggressive efforts to stop the marches and the university enrollments, and the incendiary nature of the demonstrations on both sides.

Perhaps these events, as well as the better understanding of the conflict, caused the President to make a powerful televised speech in June, 1963, in which he said that the country and its citizens face a "moral crisis." Bobby was certainly influential in this talk to the nation: he had been proposing that this be done for some time.

Also at the urging of Bobby and others in and out of the administration, Jack proposed in the June, 1963, address that a far-reaching civil rights bill be introduced in Congress. The March on Washington in August gave much-needed support to the measure that had not been welcomed by a number of powerful members of Congress.

Congress failed to pass such a law in the shortened lifetime of the President. John F. Kennedy had come from hesitance in the face of opposition to the point of actively working for ultimate laws that would protect all Americans in employment and political participation. Bobby was there in his official and unofficial roles pushing forward, at least in the latter days of the administration, with the same passion that he brought to securing the election of his brother. Their efforts at attaining the laws they desired, while unsuccessful before events led to the

Lyndon Johnson presidency, at least helped pave the way for their passage in the new administration.

Bobby served, supported, and protected his brother in the eventful 1961 to 1963 presidency in a variety of other events and situations, such as the events leading up to the war in Viet Nam; dealing with experienced public figures such as J. Edgar Hoover, Director of the Federal Bureau of Investigation; and in a variety of personal matters which Jack seemed disposed to become involved. The latter included well-publicized associations with women and with the taking of medications, in both of which Bobby urged moderation.

How the relationship of RFK to JFK adds to the understanding of Second Fiddles.

Outside forces can have a powerful influence upon the relationship of the Second Fiddle to the Principal. Here, in addition to family political tradition, the influence of the father, Joe Kennedy, Sr., set the pattern and tone for especially the boys in the family. As soon as they were old enough, the young males were to seek significant political office and to assist one another in attaining this goal. Joe, Sr., was committed to furnishing money for the campaigns and expected his children to expend their funds. He was committed also to working for the son's election publicly or behind the scenes. He assisted in creating the myths that enhanced the perception of the capability and vigor of members of the family.

At nearly every stage of demands placed upon Bobby Kennedy to manage a campaign or to serve in high office, he was reluctant to do so. A variety of motivations lay behind this reluctance. Socializing and glad-handing were not a large part of his personality. At times, as when asked to be Attorney General, he feared that the appointment might hurt Jack. When asked to head up political campaigns, he had to put aside his own goals and sometimes leave a position that gave him personal satisfaction and challenge. In the end his hesitance and his own well-being were expected to give way to service to the family and to his brother.

Though younger, Bobby came to certain conclusions on political and social issues before Jack. Bobby was then in a position, partly because of his passion for a subject, such as civil rights, to encourage and prod Jack into taking action that Jack was not yet ready to take. While other advisors and associates might be similarly pushing Jack, Bobby was typically so close by that his views were especially convincing.

The brothers' relationship was a two-way street. Jack performed the supporting role on occasion. As a member of Congress, he joined an investigating committee where Bobby had a significant staff position, with the view of supporting him in his work, or at least seeing that he did not go overboard in his pursuit of wrongdoers. And, some observers have said the attributes generally given to Bobby were actually those of Jack, and vice versa. Arthur Schlesinger suggested that Jack was a realist generally perceived as a romantic, and that Bobby was a romantic in the guise of a realist. Bobby in his passion for a cause gave the impression of hard charging, not taking prisoners, to the point of bravado, when in reality he was often unsure and holding himself together for the sake of his brother, his family, or his cause.

Bobby served as an alter ego to his brother in Jack's presidency. Part of this was caused by the position RFK held as

Attorney General, in addition to a long, very close association and the development of common goals. Bobby was the ultimate of the staff person standing in for their leader. When Bobby spoke, it was taken the same as if Jack was speaking.

Finally, although younger, Bobby assumed the role of protector of Jack and the family in ways that reflected past, present, and future. What Jack had done that might be subject to criticism was covered over. Criticism and potential harm was deflected. Divergent voices among advisors and associates were stilled. When a program or plan of action was agreed to, all involved were expected to be on board to see it through.

As to the future, the legacy of the family, its members, and the office holder at the time need to be preserved and enhanced. The family was an organism that had existed over time and was to be nurtured and treated well. After all, soon another member would be taking their place in offering themselves for important political office. Then all things had to be set that would guarantee success. And, part of this scheme would require that someone step up to be a Second Fiddle.

7

Ruth and Naomi

It is not what you think. "It" is the pledge of "Whither thou goest..." that one hears time and time again at weddings and other occasions in which someone declares their loyalty to a friend or lover. For "it" was not a passage between such intimates but rather, of all things, a vow of a woman to her mother-in-law. This certainly runs contrary to the unending parade of mother-in-law stories and jokes, in which the mother-in-law fares badly.

Following is the full passage as found in the Book of Ruth in the Bible, after the mother-in-law, Naomi, has told Ruth to return to her people: "Entreat me not to leave you or to return from following you; for where you go I will go, and where you lodge I will lodge; your people shall be my people, and your God my God; where you die I will die, and there will I be buried. May the Lord do so with me and more also if even death parts me from you."

While the words seem fresh even today, they are of ancient origin. Rabbinical and other scriptural scholars have given various dates for both the time of Ruth and the writing of the book. The reference to "When the judges ruled Israel..." in the introduction is of some help, for that occurred approximately between 1370 and 1041 B.C. The writing taking place in the fifth or fourth century, B.C. This date of the writing varies with some Jewish tradition that holds that the Book of Ruth was written by Samuel.

The Book of Ruth has long been considered a gem. It is one of the two books in the Bible named for women, the other being Esther. Ruth was noted in the old rhetoric handbooks to be "the perfect example of the simple narrative." (*The Interpreter's Bible*, vol. 2, 829) Goethe declared it to be "the loveliest, complete work on a small scale."

The story

During the time of the Judges, when there is a famine in Israel, Naomi and her husband and two sons go from Bethlehem, just south of Jerusalem, to Moab. Moab was the land of the descendants of Lot and was a long-time enemy of Israel.

Naomi's husband died, as did her two sons, survived by their wives, Orpah and Ruth. Naomi and her Moabite daughters-in-law had nothing after losing their husbands, so Naomi decided to return to Bethlehem where she had relatives and friends, and (perhaps) property that had belonged to her husband. She told Orpah and Ruth to stay in Moab with their families as she had nothing to offer them. After some convincing Orpah remained, but Ruth, giving the eloquent "Entreat me not" speech, accompanied Naomi on the journey to Bethlehem.

Because they have nothing Ruth offers to glean the barley left for the poor in the fields of the wealthy Boaz. Boaz notices her and provides her with grain to take with her at the end of the day. Naomi comes up with a plan for Ruth to be provided for—by advising her to lie at the feet of Boaz while he is sleeping and to ask when he awakens that he "spread his skirt over her." Boaz agrees to marry Ruth, and as a kinsman of Naomi's husband, further agrees to see that lands belonging to the husband are restored to Naomi.

In order to obtain redemption of the land a nearer relative to Naomi's husband must be given first right of redemption. This relative refuses because it will endanger his own children's rights of inheritance. Boaz then redeems the land and marries Ruth. They have a child Obed, who is by law the successor to the name of Ruth's first husband. Naomi nurses the child and thus has a family and a descendant for both her deceased husband and herself. Obed, Ruth's son, was the father of Jesse, and the grandfather of David. He is therefore a link in the direct line of Jesus.

Naomi and Ruth

While the story of Ruth and Naomi is known for its lessons in loyalty and trust, and the friendship between two women, it is much more. It explores anticipation and disappointment, danger and intrigue, and the relationship among women and men in that earlier era. The laws of the nation and its people come into play, and the end results are often-quoted moral and biblical truths.

The point of view of the Jews and the Moabites differed substantially. Jewish men and women were to have equal status, but each gender was given its own responsibilities. These obligations were set forth, for instance, to Moses on Mt. Sinai. Naomi and Ruth were important in their own right. Naomi was one of only four women given in scripture as being in the lineage that stretched from Abraham to Jesus. According to Jewish tradition the Messiah would descend from Ruth. She was an unlikely candidate for this role, as she was not a Jew but came from the enemy of the Jews, Moab. Moabites, contrary to the monotheistic Jews, had a polytheistic religion, based upon nature and the extensive role of goddesses, where licentiousness prevailed.

This period in Jewish history "when the Judges ruled" was a time before the kings of Israel, a rather dark period when people's attention was fixed upon their property rather than worship of their god. The story of Naomi and Ruth provides an episode of light in this time of darkness. The leading cause of light given forth by Naomi and Ruth is the selflessness of each to the other.

While Naomi fulfills the role of Principal in this classic relationship it will be apparent that there are times when Ruth takes some leadership during these difficult occasions when each is firmly reliant upon the other. Even in the initial decision to make the journey together from Moab to Bethlehem, each woman aims for the betterment of the other. Naomi instructs both Ruth and Orpah, her other daughter-in-law, to return to their families, thinking she has nothing to offer them in Israel. Ruth refuses, only after Naomi makes a second effort to persuade her. Orpah, who, according to tradition, was the ancestor of Goliath, obeyed and returned. Thus both younger women were respectful to Naomi and essentially obedient in their own way.

In making the well-known oath to Naomi, Ruth says and agrees to a great deal. Ruth asks Naomi not to require her to leave and go back home, perhaps thinking that if Naomi insists, Ruth will be bound to obey.

Ruth promises to go where Naomi leads and to live (lodge) in that place. Ruth does not know what it is like in Bethlehem, Naomi's destination. She does not know whether Naomi's "people", whom she says will be hers will accept her, a foreigner from an enemy land.

She promises to worship Naomi's god, which she probably already has learned from Naomi, is much different from that entity which she has worshipped all her life. And the oath to Naomi has the finality that includes loyalty even to their deaths. Altogether, these covenants are an abundant bundle of promises for any one person to make to another, especially considering the new territory, people, customs, and religion Ruth will be adopting.

When Ruth says she will go to Bethlehem, Naomi begins planning for a secure future for her. Naomi will begin with the basics in life, especially food, and move on to protection, land, marriage, and family for Ruth. Naomi instructs Ruth to go to fields near Bethlehem and engage in the right that Jewish law gives to widows and the poor—to glean. That is, she may pick up the remnants of the grain harvest that is left in the fields.

The fields are farmed in common, as was the custom even through feudal times. She gleans in the section of the acreage that belongs to Boaz, a person of substance who is older than she, probably the age of Naomi. It is now the time of the barley harvest, probably in April. Upon noticing her Boaz provides protection for her while she is gleaning and gives her extra portions of grain to take back to Naomi, whom he knows and respects.

Ruth's contact with Boaz prompts Naomi to come up with the next step in her program for Ruth's future. This step requires her to weave deftly through the intricacies of Jewish law and local custom. Naomi learns that Boaz will be spending the night sleeping on the threshing floor and guarding his grain harvest. She urges Ruth to lie at Boaz's feet while he is sleeping and asks him to spread his skirt over her. This equivalent of proposing marriage to the older man may have worked only at this time because it was harvest time, and the rules of propriety were said to be less stringent then. Commentators indicate that no immorality occurred in the episode of Ruth and Boaz on the threshing floor.

When Boaz agrees, the next set of complications comes into play. He is not the nearest relative to her deceased husband. This is important because marriage and the restoring of her late husband's lands are bound together. The redemption of the lands is important because it will mean that the property and line of the deceased husbands of both Naomi and Ruth will be perpetuated. Ruth and her children will have a future, as will Naomi. Naomi's role is planning and Ruth's is doing. Both contributions are necessary and so blur the lines between who is the Principal and who is the Second Fiddle. Who is more important in the relationship and their responsibilities? Their situation has been described as that of women as against the traditional male hierarchy and rules of the day. In this light they may be seen as more of a team than separate entities.

Two issues complicate matters further. In the first place, the redemption of the land inherited by her deceased husband, Mahlon, will carry with it her hand in marriage. And, not so incidentally, the first child of the marriage will be an heir of Mahlon, not Boaz. Future children after the first will be heirs of Boaz. This is another boon for Naomi since the first child will also perpetuate the line of her late husband and prevent his being the last to have his family name.

The second issue that occurs is the existence of a kinsman who is a closer relative to Ruth, through her late husband, than is Boaz. This relative, therefore, according to the law, has first right to claim Ruth and redeem the property. Neither relative is close enough that there would be any problem of incest. Boaz contacts this relative with the request that he, the relative, redeem the land. The kinsman refuses because the requirement that he marry Ruth would cause that kinsman to divide his property between the firstborn of him and Ruth, and his other children.

Boaz seals the deal over the redemption of the land by using the prevailing custom of removing his shoe and putting it back on. He does this in front of ten witnesses to confirm the transaction. Ten was a typical number to approve a marriage. In his use of the various provisions of the law of the day Boaz manages to marry Ruth without losing the support of the people of the community.

The first child born to Boaz and Ruth is Obed, who is considered to be in the line of the late husbands of Naomi and Ruth, and who will perpetuate their names. Obed is therefore a gift to Naomi, and for this the women in the story consider Ruth to be more to Naomi than seven sons would be. Seven sons in a family were considered perfection so this was quite an accolade. The women also see Obed as a provider for Naomi in her later years.

The message of the Book of Ruth

In addition to those commentators who have labeled this book as simply a good story, others have made elaborate suggestions about the purpose and message of this book. In the first place it may represent an expansion of God's plan for Israel to include Gentiles as well as Jews, foreigners as well as residents, and women as well as men. Ruth represents all of these groups who had been considered in a less favorable light. In spite of this, due to her selfless behavior toward Naomi, her conversion to Judaism, and her production of an heir in the line of David, she provides by example an argument for inclusiveness rather that rejection. While she is not a significant person in a significant era, she shows that one such as herself can make a major lasting contribution. Of course, Naomi takes the first step in accepting both of her Moabite daughters-in-law. Her argument to them that they should stay in Moab with their families was her way of supporting what she thought was in their best interests, when she thought herself to have little to offer them.

Some writers have said that God's plan was carried forth by both Ruth and Naomi through their keeping faith in him and with each other. Ruth is said to meet the qualifications of the virtuous woman found in Proverbs 31:10. Ruth and Naomi are vital links in the genealogy of the Hebrew line from Abraham to David and on to Jesus.

Practical applications of the message in this book include the encouragement of the male relative to provide an heir for a deceased man by marrying the man's widow.

Also, the story has been interpreted as an argument for foreigners to be included in the greater community of Israel, since David, the greatest king of Israel, had foreign blood.

Second fiddle—Ruth or Naomi?
At first glance at this story Naomi was surely the Principal, that is main, individual, and Ruth was certainly the Second Fiddle, her associate. After all Naomi was the older, the

mother-in-law, the initiator (at first), the planner, the person acting in place of a parent to Ruth. Ruth was younger, a daughter figure, the follower in adopting Naomi's land, people and religion. Certainly these respective roles would continue throughout their relationship.

Naomi initiated the trip back to her home and tried to talk Ruth and Orpah out of accompanying her. When Ruth chose to follow Naomi, Naomi showed that she wished to do what she could for Ruth's secure and happy life. Naomi planned Ruth's future—the means of achieving a successful husband, the way of perpetuating Ruth's late husband's name and line, and an eventual child that would continue a proud Jewish genealogy.

Ruth, on the other hand, was a follower—"Whither thou goest, etc."—content to go to a land, a people, a religion that she knew only from Naomi. She followed in trusting devotion.

Ruth did what she was told—gleaned, seduced (apparently without immorality), and proposed marriage, taking advantage of the unique circumstances provided by harvest time customs. She worked to regain Naomi's late husband's (and Ruth's late husband's) lands and lineage, even though both this maneuvering and the landing of Boaz as a husband must have been fraught with nervous and strained moments. Ruth bore a son Obed, who would secure Naomi's later years and give Naomi a prominent place in Jewish genealogy.

So the evidence is there for Naomi-Principal and Ruth-Second Fiddle. But a funny thing happened on the way to Bethlehem. Even though Naomi initiated the journey, Ruth gave Naomi strength and helped to remove the bitterness that had resulted from her loss of husband and sons. Ruth did this through a level of devotion that has been legendary for centuries. In response to Naomi's suggestions on how to secure food, Ruth worked until dark in the fields, exposing herself to serious danger from the farm workers, with little recourse as a foreigner. When Naomi wove plans for Ruth's obtaining a good husband, getting lands restored, and securing the future, Ruth took the risks and carried off the intricate details required for success.

A basic characteristic of Second Fiddles is importance to their Principals. This importance may be derived from a variety of contributions, including friendship, moral and other forms of support, and protection. Sometimes, close study reveals a near thing when judging which of the actors is more important to the other.

While the relationship of Naomi and Ruth would suggest a case for reversing the initial calculation and calling Ruth the Principal and Naomi the Second Fiddle, the abundance of evidence supports Naomi as Principal. Probably no other instance of the relationship of Principal and Second Fiddle requires each participant to perform their roles in order for each to survive. In the end, no matter which way one sees the relationship, most would agree that Naomi and Ruth, or Ruth and Naomi, constitute an unforgettable story of both devotion and action.

8

Tonto and the Lone Ranger

Several generations came to recognize "The William Tell Overture" and the shout, "Hi-Yo Silver, Away," as signs that the Lone Ranger is on the trail again. For forty years beginning in 1933 this program was on radio and then television. Since then the stories have been revealed in movies, comics, books, and other media.

Its immense popularity through the years has been verified by listeners—millions who belonged to clubs in the forties, and ate cereal and sent in boxtops for decoder rings to show their loyalty. Numerous distributors have done well in hawking merchandise related to the various programs and movies. And then comes a modern movie in 2013 featuring the famous cowboy and companion.

All this homage has been paid in spite of the fact that there was no killing, the Lone Ranger was to be almost always serious, and the program was initially designed to instill good behavior in youngsters. Parents have, of course, supported this theme of responsibility in their children.

In addition to this emphasis on morality that permeated especially the early radio version, an even more important thread has been woven through the programs in the various media—the relationship between the avenging rider in the white hat on the Great White Horse Silver, the Lone Ranger, and his Native American sidekick on Scout, Tonto.

This enduring tale of mutual support and loyalty provides another facet of the way that Second Fiddles relate to their Principals, and also the blurring of the dividing line between each entity.

First, however, it is necessary to take a close look at the story from which these two characters of American fiction have emerged.

Here's what happened

(as described by David Rothel in *Who Was That Masked Man?*)...The Butch Cavendish gang of outlaws are robbing and frightening Texas townspeople and travelers. Six Texas Rangers go with a scout to apprehend the gang, but through the treachery of the scout they fall into an ambush by the gang. Four rangers are killed and only the dying Captain Daniel Reid and his younger brother remain. The younger brother promises the Captain that he will look after Daniel's wife and their son, Danny, who are coming from the East. The gang waits at a distance and then moves on, convinced that all of the Rangers are dead.

That night a Native American visits the site of the massacre and finds the younger Ranger barely alive. He takes the Ranger to a nearby cave, tends his wounds, and remains with him during several days of fever and delirium. When the Ranger is stronger, his caretaker tells him that he is the "lone Ranger." The Ranger recognizes his companion as Tonto, who says that the Ranger saved his life when they were boys. At that earlier time Tonto had called him "kemo sabe," meaning faithful friend.

The Ranger is concerned that the Cavendish gang will look for him, but Tonto says that he has made six graves to make the gang believe that all six men are dead. The Ranger vows to seek out the gang and avenge the loss of the Rangers. He makes a mask from his brother's black vest and calls himself the "Lone Ranger." In the television version he vows to work to establish law and order on the frontier, seeking out badmen and bringing them to justice.

He starts by joining with Tonto and hunting down the members of the Cavendish gang and turning them over to the law. The fame of the Lone Ranger grows and the people of the West come to know of his trademark—the silver bullet. The silver came from a mine that was owned jointly by him and his deceased brother.

The two partners run onto the trail of Butch Cavendish, the only remaining member of the gang that killed the five Rangers. As they close in on him, the Lone Ranger's horse is shot out from under him, and he and Tonto proceed on foot, with Tonto's horse Scout carrying their gear.

A digression in the story occurs while they obtain a horse, a Great White Horse, which will play a role in their further adventures. They have heard of this legendary stallion running wild in Wild Horse Valley. They spy this mighty steed as they approach the Valley, but their trail is never an easy one. A huge bison is in mortal combat with the horse and about to get the better of the match. As the bison makes its final charge the Lone Ranger blasts away with both guns and the beast goes down.

Our hero moves to check the wounds of the big horse and finds them to be very serious. He and Tonto minister to the needs of that magnificent animal and gradually support his return to majestic splendor. When he tries to put a saddle on the horse, he bolts away. The Lone Ranger, respecting the stallion's desire for freedom, decides to let him go back to free ranging. After standing off in the distance for a time the horse suddenly bolts back to the side of the Lone Ranger.

Tonto contributes to the legend of this great stallion by saying that he looks like silver. Silver is adopted as his name as the Lone Ranger patiently trains him for the future demands of the trial that will be placed upon him.

The story continues as the two companions seek out again the trail of Butch Cavendish. The outlaw urges his horse on to outrun the mighty Silver, but his efforts are futile, and he is captured and turned over to the law for punishment.

After securing the last of the gang in jail the Lone Ranger briefly considers his future. He decides that such pursuits as ranching or mining for silver are unsuitable when placed alongside the need that he has discovered in his travels—to rid the West of badmen. So the legend of the Lone Ranger and Tonto, and their horses Silver and Scout grows throughout the frontier. They become the symbols of law and order for the peace-loving citizens moving onto the plains.

The program

The Lone Ranger program came out of the Depression. George W. Trendle, the operator of a Detroit radio station, WXYZ, needed to develop a local program in order to save his station from going under. He considered the type of program that would suit best and decided, largely on the basis of economy, that the program should be a drama, in which local actors could perform adequately; should be for youngsters, easier to please and less apt to evaluate carefully; and should be a Western, onto which radio merchandising could attach. Trendle hired a writer, Fran Striker, who had experience writing the desired type of program, and Striker performed dedicted service for the station for many years.

According to the format initiated, the hero should be a wholesome type and something on the order of Robin Hood or Zorro. He would wear a mask, use silver bullets, and have a white horse shod with silver shoes. He would have a companion to converse with in the radio episodes so as not to have to talk with his horse. The companion would be a Native American named Tonto, who would be introduced on the tenth program.

The program began on radio January 30, 1933, with the familiar "Hi-Yo Silver, Away!", and the "William Tell Overture." The music emphasized the energy of the full opening lines: "A fiery horse with the speed of light, a cloud of dust and a hearty Hi-Yo, Silver, Awa-a-ay!" Equally familiar were the last lines of each episode—"Who was that masked man?" "That was the Lone Ranger!" These lines were not added until after the program had been on the air for some time.

The Lone Ranger was broadcast fifty-two weeks a year, and written by Fran Striker and a small group of writers. The station acting group performed the program live at 7:30, on the east coast, 8:30 in the Midwest, and at first 10:30 in the west. Later the latter two programs were taped. The stories typically involved, in addition to the parts of the heroes, a juvenile leading character, a younger female lead, a female character actress, and several male characters. The leading performers were always there, except for illness or vacations, and the other roles were performed by the group of studio actors. These actors were required to maintain the fast pace of the program, a difficult skill to master for someone new.

All of the actors performed around a single microphone, and at first did their own sound effects. When sound effects people were hired, at first they shared the mike with the actors. Sound effects had to be created as demanded by the story line, and had to be injected into the story at precisely the right moment.

George W. Trendle developed a set of quite definite rules for the writers to follow. For example, the Lone Ranger was to be a model for youngsters by not smoking, swearing, or drinking alcoholic beverages. He was to use proper grammar and be gentle as well as strong. He was never to shoot to kill and was to harm even the bad guys as little as possible.

A writer's guide was written for the program and provided, among a long list of instructions that the writing should be at an adult, not a children's, level; however, the action should be maintained throughout the program. It should not be loaded with just talk. The Lone Ranger should not use heroics that were unbelievable—he was to be as normal a person as possible.

The response to the program was very dramatic. Radio stations all over the country picked up the program until in 1939 they numbered 140 stations. The Lone Ranger was mobbed in personal appearances. Sponsors, often baking companies, were very loyal in their support. In the first year, 1933, when 300 popguns were advertised, nearly 25,000 youngsters sent in requests for them.

Perhaps the best measure of the response was the myriad of promotions and merchandising that accompanied both the radio and television versions. These commercial ventures reached seventy million dollars in 1952. Over the years over seventy companies produced products to accompany the various Lone Ranger productions.

Membership in the Lone Ranger Safety Club offered to youngsters who promised to use the bread of the sponsor and get others to do likewise. In return members were given cards, codes, and badges. Membership reached two million in the Club. Close to the hearts of youngsters in the radio years were the promotions which required the mailing of a box top of Kix or Cheerios cereal, along with a dime, to General Mills. They received in this and other offers such prizes as masks, silver bullets, atomic bomb rings, and Lone Ranger Victory lapel pins.

The popularity of television dealt a severe blow to radio programs such as the Lone Ranger. The last episode, "Cold Spring Showdown," number 2596, was broadcast September 3, 1954. In the same year the television Lone Ranger was first shown.

The television Lone Ranger was played by Clayton Moore, a well-built actor and former stuntman. He became the Lone Ranger in the view of the public for many years through television, movies, and personal appearances. Jay Silverheels was chosen for the role of Tonto. He was a full-blooded Mohawk, raised on an Ontario reservation. He was an actor as well as a talented athlete, quiet, but with a good sense of humor.

The television version followed the good-triumphs-over-bad format of radio, to the extent that watching by the children was supported by their parents. In fact, more adults than children watched the show. In the 1956–57 season color was introduced to the production as well as a larger budget and the shooting of episodes on a wider variety of locations. The programs were shown on ABC on Thursdays with reruns on CBS on Saturdays.

The radio and television programs and their actors received huge volumes of fan mail, indicating that the popularity continued during the entire run. The radio and television programs also won significant numbers of awards for the quality of their programming. The promotions and merchandising likewise were sustained, and continued during the other formats of production such as serials and movies. An interesting statistic, according to some very patient counter, was that although the Lone Ranger never killed anyone, he fired over 12,000 bullets (silver, of course) at wrongdoers.

Numerous productions were spun off from the radio and television programs over the years. Examples included a play performed by the radio actors in a Detroit theatre in the early 1930's and even Lone Ranger sheet music and songbooks. Republic Studios produced two movie serials, *The Lone Ranger* and *The Lone Ranger Rides Again* in 1938 and 1939. Of course, as with other serials, each episode ended with some frightening event so that kids would have to return the following week to see how it turned out. The serials varied so far from the original plan for the Lone Ranger story that George W. Trendle would not permit motion picture treatment of the adventure for the next ten years.

In addition to a version of the story appearing in one of the Whitman Publishing's Big Little Books, Fran Striker, the principal radio script writer, wrote eighteen Lone Ranger novels between 1936 and 1957. The publisher was Grosset & Dunlap. Striker and his staff of writers also produced daily Lone Ranger cartoon strips that reached three hundred newspapers in 1954. Lone Ranger comic books were published by Dell, selling for a dime. They reached a rate of sales of two million copies a month in 1954.

After the Lone Ranger show was sold in 1954 to Jack Wrather, a Dallas oil and television entrepreneur, Republic Studios produced two movies, *The Lone Ranger* and *The Lone Ranger and the City of Gold*, in 1955 and 1958. The movies starred Clayton Moore and Jay Silverheels in the featured roles. The Wrather corporation also permitted animation companies to produce television cartoons from 1966 to 1969. In 1980 an animated half hour was shown on Saturday afternoons as part of The Tarzan-Lone Ranger Adventure Hour.

In 1980 the movie *The Legend of the Lone Ranger* was released by Jack Wrather and others and starred Klinton Spilsbury, a former photographer in the title role and Michael Horse, who had been an artist, as Tonto. Horse's Native American name was Yaqui which means dreamer of horses.

Tonto and the Lone Ranger

The relationship between Tonto as Second Fiddle and the Lone Ranger as Principal developed in the context of the efforts of the producers and writers of the radio and television Lone Ranger to introduce an action program that would incorporate lessons of patriotism, decency, and strength mixed with kindness. These emphases would be appropriate for the children who listened to or watched the episodes, would meet the approval of parents, and at the same time lead to sponsors and sales of merchandise that would make money.

In spite of the maturity of the Lone Ranger and Tonto the emphasis in the program as it was presented over the air was centered on children. This emphasis was accomplished not only by offers of items such as rings and secret codes that were attractive to the youngsters, but also the introduction of a young boy into the story line. This was Dan Reid, nephew of the Lone Ranger and son of the Lone Ranger's brother, also Dan Reid, who was killed by the Butch Cavendish gang. Before he died the elder Dan Reid asked his brother to look out for his wife and son who were on their way from the East. The Lone Ranger, after seeking his nephew for years, is dealing with a group of bandits that are trying to rob an old lady, Grandma Frisby. He subdues the robbers and comforts Ms. Frisby, who is dying of heart failure. She asks him to look after Dan, Jr., a lad of about fourteen, and tells him that Dan is not her grandson but rather was rescued by her as a baby. His mother had been killed in a Native American massacre of occupants of a wagon train. The Lone Ranger promises to care for Dan and tells Dan that he is actually his, the Lone Ranger's, nephew.

After this revelation Dan with his white horse, Victor, appears in numerous episodes of the story. He is a normal boy who, in spite of getting into occasional mischief, is respectful and polite, again emphasizing the wholesome content that was intended in the program.

In spite of the efforts to promote good behavior and strong moral character Tonto and the Lone Ranger provide, at least initially, a significant mismatch between the Second Fiddle and the Principal. Tonto was introduced as someone for the Lone Ranger to talk to—to share thoughts that would move the stories along. Tonto was to serve the Ranger by providing helpful Native American crafts, and healing and survival techniques. He was called a "half-breed Indian" in the first novel in 1936. He was not given a horse to ride on in the first couple of years on radio, but rather rode on the same horse as the Lone Ranger. According to a writer's guide for the radio show Tonto was to speak broken English and had the single mission of service to the Lone Ranger. Even the name Tonto has, some undesirable connotation. Tonto was reputed to be a name given by Native Americans to a Chief Thundercloud, who was a heavy drinker and acted unruly when drunk.

One of the reasons for this mismatch of importance had to do with the times during which the story was created. Even though the story setting was between the Civil War and the 1890's, the story was first produced during the Depression. This was a time of lingering prejudice, jealousy of minorities by those who were out of work, and the period of the revival of such groups of bias as the Ku Klux Klan. Equality might have been a goal of the program, but it was not evidenced by the two leading roles.

Particular to the Native Americans were an assortment of prejudices arising from various causes. Some whites saw these Native Americans as culturally inferior and deserving of their loss of life and lands in the wars for the American frontier. Stories, plays, and movies portrayed Native Americans as less than equals and the subject of ridicule. Even the childhood game of the day, Cowboys and Indians, reflected the conflict in status.

The views of Jay Silverheels and Michael Horse, who portrayed Tonto, emphasized their concerns about the treatment of Native Americans in the stories. Silverheels, a pleasant, educated individual with a fine sense of humor criticized the image of Native Americans on television and the movies. He claimed the creators of the stories knew little about the Native Americans and so relied upon stereotypical roles. In these roles the actor was to speak in a limited way and show little emotion. Silverheels became a dedicated spokesman for the benefit of Native American actors and disadvantaged.

Michael Horse, a self-styled activist for Native American rights and patriot, went to the producers of the 1980 film, The Legend of the Lone Ranger, and negotiated for the portrayal of Tonto's character. He found the producers sympathetic to his request that "faithful companion" not be used, as it sounded to him much like a dog. The producers also agreed that he could speak in his normal voice and show Tonto as more than a single-dimensional character. After obtaining concurrence from elders in the Native American community, Horse agreed to take the role.

The story of the origins of the masked man and his encounters with the Butch Cavendish gang in the 1980 *The Legend of the Lone Ranger* varied in a number of ways from the traditional tale. For instance, it included a love interest for the Lone Ranger, interaction with President Grant, and a more violent characterization of Butch Cavendish. The film also portrayed a more independent and equal Tonto with dress similar to that of his partner and a role of greater respect for him and Native Americans generally.

Through the efforts of portrayers of Tonto such as Silverheels and Horse balance was added to the character over the years, in spite of the producers' and writers' mirroring of the public biases. The stories likewise contributed to equalizing the relative status of the Lone Ranger and his companion. In an early episode Tonto saves his friend's life by nursing him back to health, a repayment for the earlier rescue of Tonto. The loyalty of the character of Tonto, plus his various admirable survival traits normally associated with Native Americans, contributed to a devoted following of Tonto as well as of the masked man. A substantial change in positions occurred in the 2013 movie, *The Lone Ranger*, in which greater emphasis is upon Tonto, portrayed by Johnny Depp.

Influences outside the Tonto-Lone Ranger story
Even though script-writing is a creative process, various influences play a role in the final product. In addition to racial bias, there are commercial considerations and station owner's written instructions that must be adhered to. With children's programming parents' expectations are also significant borders to writers' freedom.

The period of the story of Tonto as Second Fiddle from its inception to today reflects changes in attitudes among races and other groups in our society. In general, the character of Tonto was decidedly secondary in influence compared with the Principal, the Lone Ranger. While true, this imbalance was certainly not the case in their earliest meeting, where, according to the story, Tonto was totally in command when the Ranger was in serious physical trauma from the attack of the Butch Cavendish Gang. This life-saving domination lasted only until the Ranger was healed and the story moved on to their adventures in righting wrongs in the West.

This racial imbalance was expected from a large portion of the general population of the early Tonto era. It was seen in the movies of the times where the Native Americans were grouped as savages to be taken down by cowboys in the "cowboy and Indian" literature and movies. African Americans and Chinese Americans were employed, if at all, in servant roles. The resentment against the Japanese during World War II took its toll on these citizens' treatment in the parts they played.

While bias exists today, a larger proportion of Americans have experienced greater acceptance of those in minorities. This acceptance has resulted from changes in equality-enhancing laws, teaching of our history of race relations, and the actions of groups interested in fostering fairness. With respect to Native Americans, numerous sports teams have changed their names, dropping such references as "Redskins" and "Indians."

Diverse group treatment can still be found, however, in our literature and programming today. This is enhanced by the availability of media directed at these groups with diametrically opposed approaches to others in society. These splits in attitude in turn affect movies, TV, radio, and our smart phones.

Another fictional relationship is dealt with in this book, that of John Watson and Sherlock Holmes. At first glance one might be tempted to see this as a relationship of greater equality than that of the two Westerners. It is evident in the skills that the physician, Watson, brought into the relationship, along with a certain equality implied from the sharing of lodging at 221B Baker Street. But Tonto possessed significant utility as a companion because of his knowledge of survival and of tribal custom.

In addition, Tonto shared the wide open spaces in companionship with the Lone Ranger. Both Watson and Tonto provided a vehicle for conversation that helped to move the stories along, especially important to the Lone Ranger, who, as noted, otherwise might have had to talk to his horse.

Even though revered by a large segment of the younger and older public, the Lone Ranger and Tonto series were, at base, commercial ventures designed to sell time on the air. In addition items for sale were created that reflected the adventurous aura that attached to these two heroes, as well as products that encouraged especially young boys to consume the sponsors' products. Numerous other boys' radio programs in the same era used these enticements. For instance, this writer still has the prizes that he received from the fifteen-minute Tom Mix radio show sponsored by Ralston Purina. These treasured items include the decoder for secret messages, a sample of "real gold," and a nifty one-blade Tom Mix penknife. Incidentally, a knife like this figured in a *MASH* episode when Father Mulcahy, while away from camp, came upon a person choking. The priest called surgeon Hawkeye who asked if he had a knife or something similar. Mulcahy pulled out his Tom Mix single blade penknife and performed a life-saving tracheotomy. Who knows how many stories such as this abound in this country and overseas?

Another constraint on the various writers of the Tonto-Lone Ranger saga was the written instructions that guided the authors of the various episodes. These rules, no doubt influenced by parents, are described above and emphasized positive qualities for youngsters. Producers for similar children's ventures in the same era established parameters for writing. For instance, the manager of the group of writers of Nancy Drew, Bobbsey Twins, and Hardy Boys books developed a set pattern for these stories. For instance, the action at the end of each page and each chapter was to move the story forward, and in the end some adult figure was to praise the hero's or heroine's efforts, without which the day would not have been saved. This same stable of writers was engaged in updating the books as times changed, new devices became introduced, and older versions became dated. Even though earlier programs could not be reconstructed and the Tonto-Lone Ranger series remained set in the Old West, changes in language and culture from decade to decade were possible.

Still, with all the changes through the years that would contribute to equality between the Lone Ranger and Tonto, these characters in their original format remain one of the most uneven unions of Principal and Second Fiddle. The danger is that the condition of being an obvious Second Fiddle be considered absolutely necessary to the stories. The necessity of this uneven portrayal would, of course, simply feed the biases of those who read or view these revered stories of the old West.

A simpler view

While we have assumed the task here to look at the characteristics of the various combinations of Second Fiddles and Principals, it is equally important not to lose sight of the simpler view held by those youngsters who sat by their radios and television and immersed themselves in the adventures of the masked man, his companion, and his horse. They are the ones who we hear echoing the closing lines of "The Tenth Anniversary (on radio) of the Lone Ranger":

Lone Ranger—Phantom Rider! Ten years they've
        called him that—
And yet whate'er his journey or what the peril
        known
This is the truth about him—He never rides alone!
That cry of "Hi Yo Silver! There's danger now!
        Away!"
Calls forth a bright-eyed army to share it, come
        what may.
Whatever Strength is needed and faith too strong
        to fail—
Ten million boys and over, ride with him down
        the trail.

9

Timothy and Paul

When a traveler visits the ancient city of Ephesus in Turkey, they may run into a storyteller who shows them an inch-thick branch from a shrub which he calls the "narthex" plant. The visitor will wonder at the connection between the name of the plant and the term that is given to the entry halls of churches. How could they be related?

The Ephesus resident will then relate the story handed down through generations that concerns St. Paul's visits to the city centuries before. The dangers were enormous that faced this Jewish missionary who was very unpopular in his spreading a new religious belief to a non-Jewish community. In order for Paul to hold meetings with his followers he was forced to move around to a different place to speak every night. And the indicator of where the evening's meeting would be held was the placing in the ground outside of the home a long stem of the narthex.

Into this dangerous work Paul recruited a number of helpers to assist him in spreading his message not only among the Jews but also among the Gentiles, many of whom lived in remote and unfriendly areas. Paul's favorite of the men he chose to serve with him was Timothy.

Timothy was a native of Lystra, a remote Roman garrison in the province of Galatia. Galatia was in the general area of modern-day Ankara, in Turkey. Paul had visited Lystra when Timothy was young. Paul knew Timothy's mother Eunice and grandmother, Lois. Eunice was Jewish and Timothy's father was Greek. Timothy presumably attracted Paul's notice because of the younger man's dedication to the early church.

Paul's ability to recruit Timothy and others, in the face of the dangers of the times, to be advocates of the new religion was made even more unlikely considering the path that Paul's life had taken from the time of his early training.

Paul

This first century Apostle of Christianity was born in Tarsus in Cilicia, now Turkey, and raised in the strict Jewish tradition. He studied to be a rabbi, and in keeping with the custom of the times, also learned the tent making trade as a means of supporting himself. As a Pharisee, the Jewish group which oversaw the adherence to the Law of Moses, he became a leading persecutor of the nascent body of Christians. While engaged in this anti-Christian activity he was confronted by a vision of Jesus while on the road to Damascus.

As a result of this episode he became a fervent convert to Christianity. From his home base in Antioch in Syria, he spent the rest of his days in travel to many lands, especially among the Gentiles, to universalize the budding religion. For instance, he traveled to Galatia, Macedonia, Athens, Corinth, and Ephesus. As a result of his evangelizing endeavors he suffered in many ways: arrests, trials, imprisonments, beatings.

Through his writings which included half of the Book of Acts and a third of the New Testament, he influenced generations of adherents to Christianity. Numerous later writers carried forward his sentiments, including St. Augustine, Martin Luther, and John Calvin.

While little is known of the birth and death of Paul, his life is illuminated largely by his writings. It is also through Paul's writings we learn to know his most trusted disciple, Timothy. While Paul comments on Timothy and the nature of their relationship in other books of the New Testament, this relationship is to be learned largely through Paul's first and second Letters to Timothy.

Before going forward it is necessary to consider an issue that may not relate so much to the content of Paul's letters to Timothy as to the question of whether it was Paul who actually set this content down to writing. Of course, it is impossible to say with certainty what happened centuries ago, but it is important to look at the various positions taken by students of Paul.

Did Paul write the letters to Timothy?

The general conclusion among students of the Pauline writings is that Paul did not personally write the Pastoral Letters to Timothy. Although this is the prevailing view the problem has its complications and the answer is not as clear as it might seem. The numerous arguments for someone other than Paul to have written the letters give rise to countervailing suggestions.

One of the principal points made against Paul's authorship is that the language of these letters varies from Paul's other writings. Not only is a rather different vocabulary used but differences in sequence of words and other technical matters are pointed to. On the other hand, letters to Timothy were to a friend, not to churches, so would call for a different way of wording one's thoughts. Further, it was common practice in the time of the Apostle for scribes to write the ideas of their patrons. Of course, the various scribes would account for different patterns of language.

Another objection was that events of Paul's life were included in the Pastoral Letters that were not present in Acts, which gave a basic rundown on the life of the Apostle; however, Acts did not include all that became known of Paul's travels.

Scholars have offered various other reasons for someone other than Paul writing these letters. They point to how the described hierarchy of the church varied from actual practice of the time. The argumentative strategy was said to change from the letters to churches to the more personal letters to Timothy. The theology differed from that of Paul's lifetime; for instance, the issues regarding the Gnostics were said to be of a later historical period. A counter to this last point was that the Gnostic matter had its infancy at the time of Paul.

The specificity of the words of Paul offer a basis for authenticity. His caring admonition to Timothy to take a little wine for his stomach and Paul's references to specific followers and other acquaintances living at the time seem to support Paul's authorship.

In seeking to bring together these opposite viewpoints some apparent middle ground has been established. It has been suggested that parts of the letters to Timothy were written by different scribes, perhaps in a later era. Even so, along with this suggestion, the point is made that these scribes' writings are based upon parts of letters that were actually written or dictated by the Apostle Paul.

It may be well, in light of this extensive and complex controversy over authorship as well as to learn more of the relationship of Paul to Timothy, to look more closely at the actual Pastoral Letters. This effort is worthwhile for the caring language used by Paul toward his "son" and principal assistant, and also for the advice given to Timothy in his work in carrying on the work that Paul considers so important.

The Bible: 1 and 2 Timothy

Paul deals with many issues in these comparatively short books of the New Testament. These issues may be grouped under the topics of advice by Paul to Timothy on how to carry out both his personal life and his ministry; instructions regarding each of the types of members, old and young, men, and women; and the characteristics of the church hierarchy and the ways they should act.

Paul gives Timothy rather extensive advice as to how he and the congregation should act in the "household of faith," the Christian community. Foremost, they must hold to the Christian principles, even to the point of enduring suffering for their ideals.

Timothy should "aim at righteousness, godliness, faith, love, steadfastness, gentleness." Stay away from unnecessary controversy and "godless chatter," because it will go on endlessly to the detriment of the church. Timothy must be impartial in dealing with both his church members and also with all levels of persons. He should pray for kings and also for the rich; however, the Christian message should lead to contentment with what one has, leading to the well-known admonition that "the love of money is the root of all evil."

In order to accomplish more Timothy should delegate the task of teaching to faithful followers. He should, like an athlete, compete according to the rules. Paul cites a farmer in invoking the importance of hard work. He says that if Timothy lives by the principles that Paul has laid out he will be a good minister.

Paul's instructions presumably apply largely to men, given the relative power position of men and women in that era. It is not surprising that very little in the way of direction is given specifically to men, other than to pray without engaging in quarrels.

Paul's instructions to women raise more concerns to many women and men today. Although the admonitions are based on that same imbalance in power, they seem far different from prevailing custom today in the developed nations. Women should be silent, serious, and temperate. They should be modest in dress.

Older widows are to be supported by her relatives. In fact, whoever does not look out for his family is worse than an unbeliever. Younger widows, on the other hand, should marry, have children, and establish households. Presumably the younger widows might not be as faithful to the congregation.

Because Timothy was relatively young he was given specific advice in dealing with specific age groups. Older men should be treated like a father and older women like mothers, and younger men and women as brothers and sisters.

With the prevalence of slavery in the Pauline era admonition was given to the slaves to honor their masters. The slaves were told to honor masters in the same congregation even more since they are not only masters but to be cherished as congregants.

Paul outlines a church hierarchy of bishops, elders, and deacons that has existed to the present time in many denominations. Bishops must conduct themselves in an exemplary way, marry only once, and not be a recent convert, a drunkard or a lover of money. He must be gentle and manage his household well.

Elders are to be honored, but, if they sin, are to be chastised before all the congregants. This is still done in some congregations and called by term "churching." Elders are not to be charged with any offense except through the testimony of two or three witnesses. The requirement for multiple witnesses has come down in our criminal law of today and is a United States constitutional requirement for conviction of treason.

Deacons are to be serious and not addicted to too much wine. They are to marry only once and do a good job of managing their children and their households.

From this study of the writings of Paul to Timothy, or at least writings in Paul's name, it can be seen by implication that Paul was placing his reliance upon this young man. In attempting to settle on the validity of Principal-Second Fiddle relationship we may go further with a look at how Paul made specific allusions to how he regarded Timothy.

Relationship of Paul and Timothy
Paul regarded Timothy in a very personal way, but also as his leading associate in furthering the Christian faith among the Gentiles. On the personal side he thought of Timothy as his "beloved child" and "true son." Paul undergirded this intimacy with advice and instructions that would occur between the closest of individuals.

Paul also gives a number of indications as to the importance he places upon Timothy as a follower who has responsibilities for being both a substitute for Paul and also for carrying out various assigned responsibilities.

Paul's having a substitute was important given the large geographical area that he covered in his starting congregations on both the European and Asian continents. After the initial establishment of the congregations there was a need for contact in order to give support and advice. Paul had a number of individuals whom he could send— Timothy was the longest-serving and the one on whom Paul placed the most reliance.

Timothy performed various tasks in Paul's stead. These included calming conflicts among the members and their local leaders, teaching the principles which Paul had advocated, receiving contributions, and bearing news of the local church groups and Paul to each other. In short, he kept the congregations on track in similar fashion as he had been instructed by Paul.

Timothy was trusted by Paul and could be sent by him to perform any task whether as Paul's substitute or not. Paul considered Timothy to be "chosen," which may have meant that Timothy was endowed by a higher power to perform the responsibilities of furthering the Christian faith.

After looking to the personal and working relationships of Paul and Timothy the task remains to consider their special way of dealing with each other in the context of the Principal to the Second Fiddle. We will consider also whether this specific relationship differs from others.

"After I go": Timothy, a substitute Principal?
Timothy was Second Fiddle to the Principal, Paul. He

was Paul's assistant; more than that he is known to have been Paul's long-standing and major assistant. He had gone through imprisonment and torture with Paul. He had been a child who had grown up under Paul's tutelage. Paul had known his mother and grandmother. He had been with Paul most of his life.

He also possessed other characteristics of many Second Fiddles. He labored in the shadow of Paul. He had the complete trust of his master. From the nature of the demands placed upon him we may infer that he would have done anything his master required.

This is not to say that Timothy was an automaton. He was committed to the same religious principles as Paul. He was willing, like Paul, to suffer bodily harm and imprisonment, in addition to derision, in carrying out his chosen work of propagating the faith.

His and Paul's relationship differed from that of most Second Fiddle-Principals'. In the first place, he was considered by Paul to be like a son. This provided a greater closeness not usually seen with Second Fiddles. Paul's thinking of him as a son might have given rise to the notion of Timothy as Paul's heir, in both a personal and professional way.

A second difference arose in the manner in which we learn of how Paul regarded Timothy: through letters. Some information came through the letters to churches, but most from the Pastoral letters directed toward Timothy. So the state of the relationship can be obtained only by inference; however, strong implications as to how Paul viewed Timothy can be seen from the manner of address, the advice and encouragement given, and from the types of tasks assigned. By noting these tasks we can assume that they were usual assignments and typically carried out.

Two caveats must be considered here. One is that the authorship by Paul of the letters to Timothy is not ironclad. The best we can say is that the letters likely included some of Paul's direct writings and that the letters were in the nature of Paul's concern for Timothy and his role in Paul's life and life's work.

The other reservation is that we do not have Timothy's response to the multitudes of tenets, teachings, admonitions, and assignments in these messages sent to him. His human reactions might not always have been of the most positive sort; however, as Paul's disciple who was committed to the same beliefs and tasks as was his master, it may be presumed that he performed his subordinate role well.

A last but important difference in the present combination of Principal and Second Fiddle was the extent to which Timothy was expected to be a substitute for Paul. This substitution was predictable given the fact that Paul was under threat of death or in prison much of the time. In fact, he was in prison at the time of the second letter to Timothy. He was not free or able to travel to where he had delegated Timothy to go, thus his admonition to carry on "Till I come."

The extensive region which Paul had assumed made it impossible for him to be in all the congregations in need of his attention. The sheer workload demanded the endeavors of many helpers, the main part of the load falling upon Timothy.

The importance of Paul in the spread of the Christian message cannot be overstated; his importance as a Disciple is well-documented. From his letters to Timothy we have the documentation of Timothy's leading follower in the very difficult work that these two men assumed for themselves.

10

Tyrion Lannister and Daenerys Targaryen

Literature, plays, shows, and films are filled with stories of seconds: Mercutio to Romeo, Samwise Gamgee to Frodo Baggins, Daffy to Bugs, 99 to Maxwell Smart, Spock to Kirk, Jeeves to Wooster, Bucky Barnes to Steve Rogers (Captain America), Trapper John to Hawkeye, Ron to Harry, Play to Kid. But the second who captured our imaginations in a new way over the past decade is none other than Tyrion Lannister, the dwarf who embodied all the humanity of the Seven Kingdoms and beyond and brought us all closer to an understanding of the down-trodden. From drunk lech to soaring intellect to sharp strategist to humble servant to compassionate adviser, Lannister, played in the HBO Series by the impeccable Peter Dinklage, commanded respect from everyone who came into contact with him, within the space of a few lines of dialogue.

When we met Lannister, he was a sad man whose reputation for drinking and reading preceded him. He was famously quoted as saying "That's what I do. I drink and I know things." As the reader and the viewer got to know him, we learned that he'd fallen in love and married a woman who turned out to be a prostitute. He had never gotten over how he had been duped and the concern he still felt for the woman who had been paid by his own father to teach him a lesson. We discovered then that he had a tender heart.

Throughout his interactions with the main characters of *Game of Thrones*, by George R. R. Martin, Tyrion Lannister develops connections, either through giving life-saving advice to Jon Snow, rebukes to his nephew, Joffrey Lannister, compliments to his future wife, Sansa Stark, or road companionship to Jorah Mormont. But the person to whom he pledges his fealty and bestows his hard-won advice is Daenerys Targaryen, the Mother of Dragons, who he aids against his own family in her quest to become Queen of the Seven Kingdoms.

Nearly killed as a slave in the fighting pits, he is brought before Dany to explain his presence at Meereen, where the future queen is staging her plans and building her armies. Lannister impresses the queen and she offers him a spot among her counselors. When she is borne away by her largest dragon for months at a time, Lannister is left to rule the newly freed city and keep peace between the former enslaved people and their former masters. He brokers a deal with a religious sect to promote the queen as a savior the freed peoples have been waiting for. Commerce and good will are restored to the city. But the masters of previously freed cities descend on Meereen and Lannister realizes that all his diplomacy cannot save it from certain collapse.

Enter Daenerys again, returned on the back of her dragon, to save the day. Lannister and she conceive a plan to destroy all rebellions by former masters in Meereen and the other cities she had freed on her way to greatness. It is Lannister who tells the surviving leader to spread the word about her after she beheads his comrades and burns their attacking fleet. It is Lannister who installs a permanent solution of leadership in the free Cities so that his queen may turn her gaze across the sea to Westeros.

In Daenerys' final chapter, Lannister devises plans that fail and, then, ultimately prevail in reaching her goal to ascend the Iron Throne of the Seven Kingdoms. But her lust for revenge proves too overwhelming and she destroys the city, and the people, at the seat of her newfound power. After this, Lannister, a man who cares for the weakest among them, can no longer support her claim and he quits his position as Hand (Second) of the Queen. She throws him in jail, where he then counsels Jon Snow on his obligation to this new world that she has created. After she is overthrown and Jon Snow is exiled, Tyrion Lannister again rises to serve as Hand of the new king, Bran Stark, who has no interest in ruling. In effect, Tyrion, the best educated man with the biggest heart in the Seven Kingdoms, becomes the ruler it has needed all along.

Lannister as Second Fiddle

Key characteristics necessary for the very survival of the Second Fiddle are versatility and adaptability. The Principal can call upon the SF to perform tasks made necessary by the demands of the day. The life of the ordinary individual illustrates this. Even persons who have no great responsibilities continually are faced with work and relationship demands that can vary from hour to hour and provide surprises.

These demands are magnified in the life of the busy Principal, and, of course, they will assign the SF at a moment's notice tasks that might have been known to the Principal days before. Then it is the job of the SF, right then, to figure out what exactly is to be done, who else needs to be involved, and how to work it into the already busy schedule of already-assigned jobs. Boundless versatility in the SF is necessary to do these things, do them well, and do them in the time that can be devoted to them.

Another needed trait of the SF is adaptability. Requirements change as the Principal ascends in the position and changes in capability, efficiency, and even personality. The Principal's moving from place to place creates a new setting and a new group of actors to relate to. And, the SF will also change with time, becoming more mature, capable, or, perhaps, burned out and disillusioned.

The need for adaptability in the SF is daunting enough when they serve a single individual, but becomes a severe test for the SF when they move from one Principal to another. Style, clarity, and temperament of the Principal change, as well as the nature of the responsibilities of the Principal, as well as the setting, from familiar to the new.

Tyrion Lannister is a small but powerful walking embodiment of both versatility and adaptability. Throughout his life from humble prospect to de facto Principal—twice—he was faced with a change at every turn. Even before becoming attached to would be Principals, conditions in his life changed through misfortune and good times. He came to be relied upon by a succession of Principals who differed in what they were trying to accomplish and therefore what they demanded of Lannister.

Indeed, even trying to list all the roles that Lannister came to play is a challenge. Perhaps a starting point is the counseling which is intertwined with all the other roles. Being a counselor is based upon the initial requirement of the SF—that of being trusted by the Principal. Somehow,

Lannister manages to gain and maintain a high level of trust with a succession of Principals that is hard to match in any list of Second Fiddles in fiction or in reality.

Planning is the essential first task in accomplishing the goals of the Principal. Of course, this was evident in the long struggle by Daenerys to become Queen, showing the reality of both gains and setbacks during the struggle. Even though support of the Principal is a typical role of the SF, not all SF's are called upon, as was Lannister, to engage in propaganda on behalf of Daenerys at the time of the burning of the fleet.

During the execution of his various Principal's plans Lannister becomes a negotiator and, with foreign powers, a diplomat. Of course, anyone who has served a prominent individual knows, that just the mention of that individual's name can open doors. To truly "get things done" as a SF they must have skills in pursuing these "things" among forces that may be hostile to them and their Principal. Examples of these strengths were found in a variety of Lannister's negotiations with representatives of the Free Cities.

Lannister achieves, twice, the ultimate role of the SF, that of de facto Principal; that is, taking the place of the Principal. This happened during the absences of the Queen, but also when the King, Bran Stark, virtually abdicated the throne. Thus Lannister became the Principal, able to exercise all the skills with all the experience gained in his service to various Principals. Being trustworthy, versatile, and adaptable had paid off.

Just as one finds various forms of intellect, personality, and experience among Second Fiddles, the physical characteristics of Lannister reminds us that such attributes are no barrier to valuable service to a Principle. It may be that in certain situations a Second Fiddle who is thought to be "different" may have an advantage in that they are not taken as seriously, until their advice is found to be welcomed and utilized.

The tender heart of Lannister is a reminder that the Second Fiddle may play a "good person" to the Principal's "bad person," as well as vice versa. Of course, this dichotomy is useful in the good cop, bad cop situations. It also provides a balance to the thoughts and actions of the Principal and may be as useful as more typical of advising.

Lannister's "connections" illustrate a characteristic that is so very helpful to a Principal. Knowing where to go and who to go to can solve many sticky situations. Hopefully the Principal will not be threatened by a Second Fiddle because the latter was better endowed with network knowledge, or, for that matter, any other knowledge that would support sound advice. Lincoln said that a lawyer's time and advice are his (or her) stock in trade. So it is with the Second Fiddle.

That Lannister came to rule the city calls to mind the possibility that the Second Fiddle can sometimes gain control. This can happen in a time of the Principal's giving up power or the Second Fiddle's just taking over. This takeover possibility should not be a surprise. The attributes that make an aide valuable may be adaptable to independence and control.

Some independence in the Second Fiddle might be useful to the Principal. The assistant may, with good connections, be able to effectively "spread the word" of information that is useful to, but not attributable to, the person in charge. Similarly, non-attributable "trial balloons" might be broadcast through the network of the assistant to determine the relative acceptance or rejection of possible courses of action.

An aide's leaving the Principal can be a real possibility that can come about through the desires of one or both of the parties. A myriad of reasons might be the backdrop for such a split, as varied as the relationships of one individual to another. One may also imagine the various repercussions that can occur, even if efforts are made to make for a smooth transition. The break-up here between Lannister and the queen illustrates the rougher end of the spectrum, while on the other end, where harmony prevails, the parties use extreme care to conclude with the fewest resulting waves being made.

Finally, in addition to the overt change in the power relationship between leader and assistant, a more subtle shift in power and control may occur without drama being attached. If an aide is to be worth much, they must be able to produce, and in this effort can speak for the boss and even go beyond the positions taken by the leader. Assistants to member of legislative bodies, for instance, are considered by some observers as being in a position to make policy in the absence of control by the Principals. And, it has been further noted that these Second Fiddles have not been elected, so do not have the authority to make independent decisions.

11

Cliff Booth and Rick Dalton

In Quentin Tarantino's Academy Award-nominated *Once Upon A Time in Hollywood,* stunt man Cliff Booth embodies the Second Fiddle. Played by Brad Pitt, who received the Oscar in 2020 for his portrayal, Cliff Booth is ruggedly handsome and takes no prisoners. While his home life is lamentable—he lives alone in a broken-down trailer with his amazingly well-trained dog, Brandy—he is the man every man wants to be. In one memorable scene, he takes on a Bruce Lee-like character in the back lot and thrashes him decisively. But he is quiet in his approach, showing no hubris, and happily takes a backseat to his leading man, actor Rick Dalton, played by Leonardo DiCaprio, for whom Booth is his lifelong stunt man and best friend.

Chauffeuring Dalton around, accompanying him to business meetings, dispensing one-line chestnuts to Dalton's constant whining about his failures as an actor, and doing Dalton's dirty work comprise the majority of Booth's interactions with his Principal. It's 1969 and Dalton's next-door neighbors are hot new director Roman Polanski and his wife Sharon Tate. The ominous presence of the Manson family interspersed throughout the poignant and comic scenes with Dalton and Booth give the film its real conflict at the heart of the movie. (In one of the film's most suspenseful scenes, Booth returns a hitchhiker to her home on Spahn Ranch, where the family lives, and challenges them. He is far outnumbered, but he escapes in style. Just the way one would hope one would if faced with a similar dilemma.)

So it's no surprise at the end that Booth defeats some members of the family in Dalton's home, while the self-absorbed actor floats in his pool listening to music. Dalton gets in on the action and helps to save the day, but it is Booth who does the heavy lifting in getting the bad guys. After the excitement, Sharon Tate invites Dalton into her home, signaling a return to relevancy for Dalton, while Booth, bloodied and bandaged, is carted away in an ambulance.

The first and last lines Booth utters in the film, in response to being told that he is a "really good friend" to Rick Dalton, are the same: "I try." The simple sentiment sums up Booth's efforts, which seem effortless when viewed a certain way, but, in retrospect, are incredibly difficult given the vagaries of Hollywood and troubles of the times. Dalton himself tells Booth he can no longer use his services after returning from months in Italy shooting spaghetti westerns and then marrying a starlet there. But Booth is steadfast and loyal through thick and thin, ultimately saving his life and his career in a single evening.

Once Upon A Time in Hollywood is a love letter to stunt men, the Second Fiddles of one of the most lucrative industries, the most creative endeavors, and the most popular forms of entertainment in the world. It's a natural for a book about people who support others, even if they break a few bones in the process.

The Second Fiddle

The roles of Stunt Man and Stunt Woman show in a unique manner many of the ways that the Principal and the Second Fiddle relate to each other. In these roles that are perhaps the most dramatic and exciting in Hollywood, the audience can take in so many of the nuances of Principal to Second Fiddle while enjoying the show. Unfortunately, except for awards ceremonies and articles about the Silver Screen, people who do stunts for a living are far in the background. Indeed, the very fact that the Star has not performed the difficult or dangerous feat required by the script is most often very hush-hush.

This relative obscurity of stunt work makes *Once Upon A Time in Hollywood* not only a seldom-seen exposure to stunts and their performers, but also feeds into the study of Second Fiddles example after example of close-ups of Second Fiddles in everyday interaction with their Principals. The necessity of inflating the interaction for purposes of motion picture action and drama causes us to see that there are many levels of relationship; these examples might be otherwise missed.

For instance, one can readily see subservience personified. The very act of the Stunt Man walking behind the actor in the movie is reminiscent of an early heritage of servant or slave, lower caste to upper, or, in some societies, woman to man. It is ironic that in this motion picture the relationship of the two men is so much more than their professional roles.

The act of chauffeuring by the Stunt Man here is another indication of subservience that is only partially explained away by the actor's having lost his license through DUI. One senses that this service on the part of the Stunt Man is just one of the many ways that he "stays close" to the person for whom he is "more than a brother and less than a wife."

Cliff Booth's determination to stay close may help to explain other actions of a servant. "I'm your gofer." He carries luggage, cares for the actor's house, and repairs his antenna. Whatever the motivation behind his performing these tasks, that performance illuminates the fairly typical demands of Principals in more formal settings to readily expect the Second Fiddle to accomplish the mundane as well as the important duties of the assistant.

Cliff's gift of perception of weaknesses and strengths in individuals, especially in his Principal, may be used to illuminate other such relationships. For instance, he sees Rick Dalton's insecurities, and takes them under consideration in his service to Rick. How often do Second Fiddles in politics, business, and other fields form their actions and responses because they see the boss's lack of confidence. One clue, of course, would be the penchant for the Principal to assign difficult or awkward tasks with a "Why don't you handle this."

An interesting and instructive by-play results when the "less than a wife" Cliff is informed by Rick that he is getting married. Further than that, Rick tells Cliff that he will no longer need his services. How does this turn of events apply to loyal and long-serving Second Fiddles when someone else is inserted into an established relationship. How does the Second Fiddle react? What are their options? In what instances do they merely "grin and bear it" because of a sense of loyalty to the Principal, their role in an organization, or their pay-check?

This leads to a dramatic situation where Cliff actually defends Rick's new wife from a deadly home invasion by the Manson gang. This defense is done without hesitation and without apparent concern by Rick in his recent displacement. What questions does this dramatic episode raise when, after being let go, a Second Fiddle has an opportunity to "fight for" their former Principal's principles or position.

And, while all this life and death fight is going on, Rick is shown to be floating in his pool, oblivious of the threat to his friend, his wife, and his own life. How often is the Principal in an important or celebrity role unaware of the "fights" that the Second Fiddles take on for them? How do the Second Fiddles react to this lack of awareness? How should they react? What duty is there upon the Principal to seek to be aware of such sacrifices?

Upon first looking at this "mere movie," one might see it only as entertainment, a piece of art, or a night at the Bijou; however, serious instruction can be found in unexpected places. If one wishes to have a thoughtful pause in looking at the division of responsibilities and sensibilities between the Second Fiddle and their Principal, various art forms are a helpful place to start.

Motion Pictures and Second Fiddles: Variations

Motion pictures provide examples of the various ways that the relationship between the Principal and Second Fiddle can go awry. For instance, the assistant may be portrayed as weak or bumbling. This is sometimes the case even when the original writing had the aide as a person of competence. A weaker Second Fiddle can even become the target of abuse by the Principal.

In looking at instructive examples of these and other deviations from the model of leader and assistant, it is well to reconsider the basic characteristics of the model relationship—one party being of real help to the other, along with the loyalty of the helper to the person in charge. While loyalty is held constant in our present considerations, we will look at some of the ways that assistance can become less than useful.

The case of the bumbling assistant is illustrated in the person of Dr. Watson in the Sherlock Holmes film series featuring Basil Rathbone as Holmes and Nigel Bruce as Watson. Watson often does not grasp the principles of detection suggested by Holmes, nor does he seem to know on occasion what is happening around him. Worse yet, he sometimes cannot be relied upon to complete an assigned task. While unflaggingly loyal, he doesn't possess the competence to be an adequate Second Fiddle.

Compare this lack of competence in this film series Watson with the characteristics in the original adventures as written by Arthur Conan Doyle. There Watson was relied upon to give his opinion on the facts of the case, but more importantly to give his expert opinion in any medical issues that would arise. He was relied upon even to the extent of being required to come armed to the dangerous situations that he and Holmes faced together.

Even when he could not as quickly comprehend the meaning of the facts of the mystery as Holmes—who could?—he was treated with respect and good nature. Consider the exchange beginning of "The Adventure of the Dancing Men," when two events puzzled Watson. One was the way in which Holmes deduced that Watson had decided not to make a certain investment. After Holmes gave his usual step by step deductions that included the presence of chalk on one of Watson's fingers, Watson's likely meeting a friend for a game of pool at his club who was selling the investment, and Watson's not obtaining his checkbook from

Holmes' locked desk, Watson considered the solution "absurdly simple." As typical, it can be noted that Holmes did not gloat but moved on to a second puzzle.

This puzzle involved a message that involved only stick figures resembling dancing men that had been received by a client's wife. Upon Holmes' inquiry Watson considered them to be merely a child's drawing, which they certainly resembled at first glance. The turned out to be anything but simple figures as the adventure progress.

In both of these illustrations Watson does not understand the issues at hand; however, the charm of these adventures is that the readers would not be able to reach a conclusion any quicker than Watson, but it is left to the superior unique deductive powers of Sherlock Holmes. Again, Holmes does not make sport of Watson but moves on to rely on the Doctor as trusted companion, and as competent aide. Here we see the contrast with the film version of the seriously confused, incompetent Watson.

The "cowboy" movie often featured a "sidekick" who was very loyal to the hero but was there mainly as a charming comic. While occasionally proving useful, he would be the lovable butt of jokes. Of course, these characteristics distinguished the Second Banana from the Second Fiddle, based upon the requirement of usefulness.

While the woman friend of the female lead sometimes exhibited this same inanity, the second woman character often played by Eve Arden and others was that of a competent individual. An alternate persona played by Ms. Arden was that of a witty pal, who sometimes saw the reality of the unfolding story before the heroine. In either case her role came close to meeting the requirements of the Second Fiddle.

Complex relationships between Principal and Second Fiddle can add interest and value to the story line of a film. For instance, in "Random Harvest" the roles of Principal and supporter change throughout. At first Ronald Coleman, wounded and with shellshock from the World War, is rescued by a dancer, Greer Garson. After their marriage he loses his memory in an accident; she becomes his secretary without his grasping that she is his wife; and she patiently serves him in the office until he finally understands their relationship in the dramatic end of the picture. Coping with the change of roles in a film such as this requires a diagram that follows the progress of the story; however, those who like challenges at the theater find the attention required to be worth the effort.

As indicated by these few examples, motion pictures and other forms of dramatic art can provide illustrations of the various formats of the Second Fiddle in relation to the Principal. And, from the axiom that art follows real life, actual examples of human relationships are all around us and yield both simple and complex models of aide to leader.

Second Fiddles and Their Principals—Ultimate Relationships

Change is a major theme of our times, sometimes accelerating and sometimes slowing. How will future changes affect Second Fiddles and their Principles? Even from the examples given here, one can see almost endless real and fictional relationships.

Real world relationships, before and ahead
Business and military leadership and support warrant extensive recognition and study. Even though a commercial venture is often identified by its CEO, aides are required to help with the numerous tasks of business leadership. The military chain of command can complicate evaluation of the various ways the auxiliary officer supports the commander.

The attitude of personal commitment to a nonprofit or religious cause may change the way that both the leader and subordinates carry out their respective tasks, with the possibility of a more "all in" attitude.

Cultural changes can affect deeply personal relationships as where a spouse or family member performs the role of assistant. The growth of independence of women, for instance, can strain a presumption of being there for the husband without concern for other ventures the women may choose to pursue. The relative ease in getting another position can affect anyone's decision to stay or go, work harder or less, be ordered around or not.

Cultural issues also affect the leadership of activities in which the public plays a significant role, such as politics, education, the media, and sport. The public may feel that they have a vested interest in these activities, and that this interest extends to looking over the shoulder of leadership and therefore the leader's way of relating to subordinates. Changes in attitudes on race and minority involvement may have an effect upon leader and aide.

Scientific progress must be considered now and in the future. The utilization of ever more sophisticated robots fosters new ideas on how the leader may be helped by other than humans. Even present-day robots are performing tasks that would be useful to the one in charge. Loyalty at first glance would seem to be taken for granted; however, present progress of these machines would predict greater independence in their actions and even in their derivative thought processes.

Past, present, and future fictional Second Fiddles

It can be seen that the relationship of leader to assistant is a very complex one, affected by personal issues, the nature of the tasks to be completed, and the cultural and other surrounding circumstances. Fictional leaders provide an endless source of reminders of these influences, from the classics onward.

It would be a mistake to be too high-brow in the selection of genre, since even what might be considered more trivial can yield instruction. For instance, what can farce with its predictable outcome teach when we encounter there a leader and helper? And, even with slapstick, it is necessary to have more than one participant, sometimes the willing long-suffering assistant, or the unwilling serving the unfit. While hilarity may ensue, the possibility for abuse is present, the examination of which might shed light on day to day encounters.

Ever-changing fictional mediums will keep the leadership student stocked with subjects. The abundant forms of presentation are altered by the times in as many ways as can be conceived by the human imagination. While some consider from time to time the written word, such as the book format, to be endangered, it seems to be holding up rather well.

The motion picture continues to evolve and portray the Second Fiddle in its present context and in the writers' visions of what is to come. Television demands more production of material for traditional and cable broadcasting and for streaming and other options being developed. Comic strip heroes and supporting casts yield a favorite form of both adult and youth entertainment.

These and other forms of presentation of fiction present an unending supply of opportunities for dissecting how the Second Fiddle relates to the Principal. And there are doubtless further forms to come. Further, the crossover of similar situations between fiction and real life help predict the future for the Second Fiddle.

In the end, when one comes across a real or fictional leader, the Principal, one would do well to look beyond that individual and determine whether, just beyond, they will find a helpful and loyal assistant, the Second Fiddle.

Acknowledgments

I am grateful for the opportunity to thank our daughters: Alice, for her belief in this concept and perseverance in its completion; and Camille, for bringing her considerable skills in the guidance and formation of this book. I also wish to thank granddaughter Kemper for her professional proofreading of this book. And I appreciate Alexia Garaventa, who contributed creatively with cover and design.

Diane read it all as she has for way over sixty years, artfully suggesting improvements and offering encouragement. And thanks to Mom and Dad for their getting my brother and me started toward contributing what we could.

About the Author

Paul C. Cline is a retired university professor who founded the Political Science Department at James Madison University. Starting at then-Madison College, Cline served as executive administrator (Second Fiddle), and, after forming the Poli Sci Department, led it through massive cultural changes. At the time of his retirement after 37 years, Political Science was one of the largest departments and the most popular major at JMU.

Cline has co-authored several books on government and law-related topics. He writes stories for the family and on local history. He served in United States Army Intelligence and practiced law for a time. He holds law and doctor of philosophy (government) degrees and has held several elected public offices, including in the Virginia House of Delegates.

Selected Sources—Second Fiddles

Alter, Jonathan. *The Defining Moment: FDR's Hundred Days and the Triumph of Hope.* New York: Simon and Schuster, paperback, 2006.

Barkley, William. *The Letters to Timothy, Titus, and Philemon*, rev. ed., in The Daily Study Bible Series. Philadelphia: The Westminster Press, 1975.

Berg, A. Scott. *Max Perkins: Editor of Genius.* New York: New American Library, 1978.

Brinkley, Alan. *John F. Kennedy.* New York: Times Books, Henry Holt and Company, 2012.

Conway, Joan. *Who's Who in the Old Testament.* New York: Bonanza Books, 1971.

DeSilva, David A. *An Introduction to the New Testament: Contexts, Methods & Ministry Formation.* Downers Grove, Illinois: InterVarsity Press, 2004.

Doyle, Arthur Conan. *The Complete Sherlock Holmes.* Garden City, New York: Doubleday & Company, Inc., 1930.

Feiler, Bruce. *America's Prophet.* New York: William Morrow, 2009.

Ferguson, Barbara P. *Joshua, Judges, and Ruth.* N. p.: Graded Press, 1988.

Friedman, David Noel, *et al.*, eds. *Eerdmans Dictionary of the Bible.* Grand Rapids, Michigan: William B. Eerdman's Publishing Company, 2000.

Goodwin, Doris Kearns. *The Fitzgeralds and the Kennedys: An American Saga.* New York: Simon and Schuster, 1987.

Heymann, C. David. *RFK.* New York: Penguin Putnam, Inc., 1998.

Holy Bible, The. Revised Standard Version. New York: Thomas Nelson & Sons, 1953.

Kushner, Harold S. *Overcoming Life's Disappointments.* New York: Alfred A Knopf, 2006.

Montville, Leigh. *The Big Bam: The Life and Times of Babe Ruth.* New York: Doubleday, 2006.

Morgan, G. Campbell. *The Unfolding Message of the Bible.* Westwood, New Jersey: Fleming H. Ravell Company, 1961.

Riggins, Walter. *Numbers.* Philadelphia: The Westminster Press, 1983.

Rothel, David. *Who Was That Masked Man? The Story of the Lone Ranger.* San Diego: A. S. Barnes & Company, Inc., rev. ed., 1981.

Rowley, Hazel. *Franklin and Eleanor: An Extraordinary Marriage.* Farrar, Straus and Giroux, 2010.

Sorensen, Theodore C. *Kennedy: His Life.* New York: Harper & Row, 1965.

Telushkin, Rabbi Joseph. *Jewish Literacy.* New York: William Morrow, 2001.

Thomas, Evan. *Robert Kennedy: His Life.* New York: Simon and Schuster, 2000.

Ulanov, Ann Belford. *The Female Ancestors of Christ.* Boston: Shambala Publications, Inc., 1993.